Feminism in West African Novel

for
my parents

Feminism in West African Novel

M. Farida Begum

Prestige
an international publishing house

Published by
Prestige Books
New Delhi 110 058
Ph. 9818755529
email: prestigebooks@gmail.com
website: asiabookclub.com
ISBN: 81-7851-053-7

Printed at Chaman Offset Press, New Delhi 110 002

Contents

I don't think I am a radical feminist. I don't even accept that I'm a feminist. I accept I'm an ordinary woman who is writing about what she knows. I try to project the image of women positively. When I do write about women in Nigeria, in Africa, I try to paint a positive picture about women because there are many women who are very, very positive, in their thinking, who are very, very independent, and very, very industrious.

Flora Nwapa

Being a woman, and African born, I see things through an African woman's eyes. I chronicle the little happenings in the lives of the African women I know. I did not know that by doing so I was going to be called a feminist. But if I am now a feminist then I am an African feminist with a small "f."

Buchi Emecheta

For us Africans, literature must serve a purpose: to expose, embarrass and fight corruption and authoritarianism. It is understandable why the African artist is utilitarian.

Ama Ata Aidoo

Preface

The book is an attempt to trace the emergence of 'new' African woman craving for economic independence, self-reliance and the readiness to combat discrimination, exploitation and victimization in patriarchal African society. African feminism as a generalized concept has the chief objective of feminism as a movement to accomplish specific tasks to bring awareness in women about their just rights in all the spheres of life of woman besides dispelling the misconception that its sole purpose is to hate male authority. Feminism as a commitment to struggle for women's liberation from all kinds of atrocities—internal, external, psychological, socio-economic, political, and philosophical and discrimination based on race, class and culture—is viewed not as a simple reform but a revolution.

Feminism from the 'feministic point of view' is a cry against male chauvinism, eternal degradation, constant humiliation and perpetual victimization. It is worth-noting that some female writers have blatantly put forth the feminist ideology while others with an underlying current and the rest have exhibited non-committal tendencies. The West African fiction sharing the vital social responsibility attempts to bring awareness in African woman that may hopefully lead towards establishing an idealized African society.

I owe a deep sense of gratitude to my teacher Dr. S.A. Khayoom, Professor and Head of the Department of English and Comparative Literature, S.K.University, Anantapur, for his invaluable academic guidance and constant encouragement during the period of my research. I sincerely thank other members of the teaching faculty for their valuable suggestions and encouragement. I am also grateful to Late Padmabhushan Prof. C.D. Narasimhaiah and Prof. C.N. Srinath of Dhvanyaloka, Mysore, for their help. I profusely thank Mrs. Azra Javed, Joint Secretary and Correspondent, Osmania College Committee, Kurnool, for her encouragement and to Janab M. Azmathullah Khan Saheb, Administrative Officer and Member of the Governing Body, Osmania College Committee and Executive Council Member, S.K. University, Anantapur for inspiring me to complete my task of research.

I express my gratitude to my dear brother M. Fazeel, M.P.D.O., for his constant inspiration and support in my academic endeavour. I make a mention of my beloveds Gudiya and Ajju for extending their cooperation to me in carrying out my research work. My special thanks are due to my beloved husband Dr. S.M. Basha, Lecturer in English, Osmania College, Kurnool, without whose help and guidance this project would not have been possible.

Chapter I

Introduction

African Literature is a twentieth century creation primarily concerned about Africa, African traditions and customs. It has attracted the audience outside Africa as well and established that Africa is no longer a dark continent and a gloomy phenomenon inhabited by witches, medicine men, wild life, cannibalistic pigmies and Tarzans—a misrepresentation and distortion of "things" African but rich in culture and mythology.

The 'new' voice of Africa, the contemporary African writing in English, has vehemently contested the western antithesis of Africa and African. It tries to emancipate Africa from its literary stereotype and complexes born of years of degradation and self-degradation. As every true literature is an art of cultural self-definition, African literature too reflects and represents native culture. It is more functional and purposeful and exploring the human condition in Africa it tries to highlight the 'unique and novel' potentialities of the man of Africa. Further, it attempts to define the world and evaluate Western aesthetics in terms of African aesthetics, culture and philosophical assumptions.

African literature has to be studied and examined in African context from the point of view of African aesthetics, politics and history. Beauty and pleasure are not the basic things as in most of the Western literature. African writing today aims at preserving African culture and African character unaffected by the outside world. Modern African literature has gained significance not for its historicity but for presenting in the more restricted and more immediate sense, the socio-cultural environment prevailing in Africa. African anthropological details are integrated into African fiction for its artistic purposes. The dichotomy of the two worlds not in opposition but as a unity has made contemporary African writing in English more alive, relevant and interesting to the Western reader.

Abiola Irele in *The African Experience in Literature and Ideology* says that the term "Africa" has a wider connotation.

> For however gratifying it might be, for the sake of intellectual rigour, to arrive at a precise definition of African literature, the effort would still be beside the point, which is to place into focus what I consider to be the essential force of African literature—its reference to the historical and experiential. It is this, which in a real and profound way justifies the ready attachment of the historical and politico-ideological connotation of the term "Africa" to such a diversity of texts and material.[1]

Abiola Irele opines that the term "African" appears to correspond to a geographical notion but in practical terms, it also takes in those areas of collective awareness that have been determined by ethnic, historical and sociological factors, all these factors, as they affect and express themselves in the literature, marking off for it a broad area of reference. Within this area of reference, and related to certain aspects that are intrinsic to the literature, the problem of definition involves also a consideration of aesthetic modes in their intimate correlation to the cultural and social structures which determine and define the expressive schemes of African peoples and societies.

Modern African writing, like modern creative writing in English emerging from the Third World countries, especially from the earlier colonies of Britain, reflects the impact of colonial experience on the native consciousness and the writers' increasing awareness of the peculiar problems confronting the individual, society and the nation at large. Colonization over the centuries in some African countries, like in several other colonies of the British Empire, has greatly affected the native sensibility. Many illogical consequences and contradictions in the society are ascribed to the impact of alien culture. Since the native society could not totally wipe out the vestiges of colonialism, African writers have adopted an enlightened outlook for a possible synthesis of the two cultures—native and western. They are deeply committed to re-educate and regenerate the society and try to redefine its traditional values.

Chinua Achebe once said that African novel had to be about Africa as a geographical expression and as a metaphysical landscape. He added that it should be about "a view of the world and all of the cosmos perceived from a particular position." Chinua Achebe's first novel, *Things Fall Apart* which has become a classic in modern African writing in English, attempts to reconstruct the fractured Igbo traditional society and redefine African cultural identity. African writer, conscious of his social milieu and the subversive impact of colonization affecting the native psyche, is committed to decolonizing the African mind. It is the bounteous duty of an African writer to sensitize African to his cultural identity and African tradition and to take pride in 'things' African. Achebe held the view that African peoples did not hear of culture for the first time from Europeans, that their societies were not mindless but frequently had a philosophy of great depth and value and beauty that they had poetry and above all, they had dignity.

On the qualifications for becoming an African novelist, he added that it is partly a matter of passport, of individual volition and particularly of seeing from that perspective. Being an African, like being a Jew, carries certain penalties as well as benefits of course. But perhaps more penalties than benefits. (Joseph Conrad of *Heart of Darkness* was a European who did not want to be an African). And it is not even a matter of colour, for Africa has Nadine Gordimer, Doris Lessing and other novelists.

Peter Igbonekwu, while discussing the essential elements of African literature, says that it gives him opportunity to project the positive image of Africa, to counter its misconception by the Western world. African novelist gives a vivid picture of Africa's past and its native traditions for better understanding of African culture and sensibility. James Ngugi Wa Thiong'o, the most exciting and powerful writer responding to most of the issues, topical and of public interest, has advocated total liberation, that is, political, economic and psychological emancipation depicting East-African situation in his works.

Anne Tibble in *African-English Literature* rightly observes that thinking briefly, of West Africa as a self-contained literary unit—which of course it is not, though cross-currents with East and South Africa are not strong, we may say that this section of the continent began its production of a written literature latest of the three. When as late as the 1940s, West Africa did awake, the number of its writers quickly grew. Especially so was the case in Nigeria, in spite of the hundred or more indigenous languages there. The total of poets, novelists, and dramatists in West Africa as a whole quickly exceeded those in the South or East.

West African fiction, as can be seen in the works of famous Nigerian writers like Wole Soyinka, the Nobel Laureate, Chinua Achebe, Cyprian Ekwensi, T.M. Aluko, Amos Tutuola, J.P. Clarke, Flora Nwapa and others, offers to the native reader and outsider to enlighten him, the most passionate expression of cultural confrontation during the colonial period and the impact of alien culture on the African psyche and the native's desire to control his own destiny in a sovereign state. The growth of literary production in Africa is ascribed to significant historical events like the arrival of white man with his culture, new faith and new 'isms'. The depiction of social, political and cultural change in Africa has made the novel more realistic and highly contemporaneous.

Chinua Achebe, James Ngugi and others have tried to analyse African experience and the nature of mutation in African society exposed to the onslaughts of the West. African writers are sensitive to the prevailing conditions of life in Africa and have skillfully dramatized the historical events to trace the growth of African consciousness. Achebe as a chronicler concerned about the historical change attempts to reconstruct the Igbo society in his first three novels—*Things Fall Apart*, *No Longer at Ease* and *The Arrow of God*. In these novels, there is a particular ordering of events to reveal a tragic pattern to record the effects of colonialism and the tragic consequences of African encounter with Europe.

African fiction in general is dominated by protest against the corrosion of traditional values by colonization, evangelization and urbanization. The people are lured by 'high-life' and money culture during and after the colonial period. Since Nigeria and certain parts of West Africa were less exposed to the onslaughts of the West, the focus in Nigerian novel is more on African cultural identity than negation of European values. The protest in Nigerian novel seems to be two-fold: against the alien culture that corrupted the Blacks and the Blacks that corrupted themselves. Achebe and Ekwensi have blamed the Africans themselves for traditional mores and weaknesses and for the rampant corruption in Nigerian society and have advocated a change initiated by African tradition and culture without the interference of alien culture and other external influences.

African novel of the nineteenth and twentieth century has generally depicted the patriarchal society dominated by male. Women in the society are relegated to a secondary place. Frank Katherine in her controversial article *Women Without Men: The Feminist Novel in Africa* encourages women to assert themselves and shape their own destiny. "The feminist writers of Africa portray women not only as taking active and shared roles with men but also as finding a destiny of their own . . . destiny with vengeance."[2]

African novel emerging from the underlying tension between the notion of pan-African unity and national identity testifies to the writers' belief that 'fiction has a vital social responsibility', and most of the material of the narrative constitutes 'charting their own social reality'. It deals with the precision and the plight of the marginalized woman struggling to sustain herself and her non-entity status and disappointments overshadowing her existence and above all the choked voice—a victim of eternal degradation and humiliation struggling hard to be heard but all this with the undercurrent of the typical African tradition and culture.

The gender discrimination that is intrinsically interwoven into the fabric of African society and the battling initiative and determination of African woman to preserve her womanhood that is viewed as her sexuality and ability to bear children against the embodied male-dominance gratifying its lust in female subordination are beautifully portrayed in the African novel. The novel depicts how the suppressed and oppressed women are sacrificed at the altar of male-oriented society and the men's exploitation of women to maintain male dominance and thus subjecting women to struggle for their self-actualization and recognition outside the domestic sphere. Even the characters in African novel without character growth represent some aspect of traditional values or vision of life.

In the traditional novels, archetypal characters are portrayed in their native surroundings. As corporate beings, they represent collective consciousness and sometimes respond individually in the changed circumstances. Because of kinship, which is the basic trait of African society, the society is coherent and organic.

Chinua Achebe's novels *Things Fall Apart*, *No Longer at Ease*, *A Man of the People* and *The Arrow of God* are concerned with the nature of mutation within the Nigerian society. *Things Fall Apart* (1958) depicts the disintegration of the hitherto self-contained society with the arrival of the white man. It is significant as it marks the beginning of the cultural conflict in African novels. The Igbo woman is portrayed as a traditional woman in patriarchal society. Women are portrayed as voiceless and unassertive in their own village dominated by males.

The novels of Chinua Achebe speak of Igbo culture, Igbo traditions and Igbo history. Igbo society is patriarchal, egalitarian, and polygamous. It is a title-society where titles are conferred to individuals based on their prowess demonstrated in wars with neighbouring clans and the number of barns of yam seed produced by the individual. It is basically a masculine society. Man without a title is disregarded in his own village. Unoka, Okonkwo's father, is called a 'loafer' in Umuofia. Only the rich could afford to marry more than one wife by paying bride price. Women do not have any say in the decision-making but have to support their family and participate in agriculture and communal activities and celebrations. For centuries, African women were considered insignificant, neglected, exploited and denigrated.

The novel suggests violent conflicts due to the utter lack of a moderating female influence. Achebe makes use of a folk tale narrating the conflict between the earth representing fertility or the female principle and sky denoting the male principle. They assert that Okonkwo's despair was due to the imbalance and insanity of the female principle," occasionally but reluctantly yields his tender emotions most often expressed perversely towards Ikemefuna and Nwoye, is a paradigm for sky who withholds rain but releases it reluctantly and perversely, since rain falls as it has never fallen before, preventing vulture who represents the female principle from returning to deliver his message just as Nwoye, with his effeminate nature, does not return to Okonkwo's compound." (*Things Fall Apart*)

No Longer at Ease (1964) shows how Africans have given themselves to the trappings of modernity in the colonial period. There is a discernible change in the style of Achebe's portrayal of female characters in his second novel. Obi Okonkwo subdues himself to the traditional ethos when it comes to choose between his mother who threatens to kill herself if he would marry Clara against her wishes, and Clara, an outcaste whom he wishes to marry. His mother represents traditionalism while Clara stands for modern feminity. Clara gets aborted and fades out of the story. She is educated, economically independent and confident of leading life without Obi Oknokwo.

In *A Man of the People* the protagonist Odili who symbolizes Nigerian educated youth is at the crossroads unable to assert himself. But Eunice as lawyer and financer of the common people's convention opposes the corrupt chief Nanga when he shoots Max, the founder of the convention. Eunice decides to retaliate. She kills the chief with her pistol. "She opens her handbag as if to take a handkerchief [takes] out a pistol instead and fires two bullets into chief Coco's chest." Achebe adds approving her action: "Only then does she fall down on Max's body and begin to weep like a woman . . . a very strange girl," people said. (160)

The Arrow of God (1966) depicts the triumph of the old order by the new order and the old faith by the new faith. Achebe as an insider gives an authentic picture of the extent of impact of Western culture on African culture, faith and African psyche.

Achebe's female characters in the first three novels are idealized women in their traditional roles but in his later novels women become active participating in nation-building activities. However, his female characters lack depth. Achebe's female characters are quite often confined to their household activities like ideal mothers. But a few women like Chielo, the priestess of the oracle of the Hills and the Caves, are respected in Umuofia and Ani, the Goddess of Earth, is worshipped by the entire community.

Ekwensi in his novels of city life depicts the life of women lured by the city attractions and high life of Lagos. His *People of the City* and *Burning Grass* deal with the clash between the ways of African rural village and those of the modern commercialized city. T.M. Aluko in *One Man, One Wife* presents the conflict between the monogamy of Christianity and polygamy of traditional society. His second novel *One Man, One Matchet* also presents similar conflict between tradition and modernity.

Ayeta Anne Wangusa's *Tears of Hope* speaks of the plight of African rural woman in traditional patriarchal society, their physical suppression and repression. Her popular novel, *The Official Wife* is critical and satirizes both polygamy and the marriage practised in the contemporary society under the influence of the West. Kehinde Ayooola's first novel, *The Running Woman* is about the struggle of a mother shouldering the responsibility of bringing up her three twins. Peter Kirman's novel, *Before the Rooster Crows* presents the economic disparities, racism and brutality in Africa and similar inequalities in other societies outside Africa.

Margaret Aogolo's *I Swear by Apollo* records the sufferings of the AIDS-affected orphans, adulthood, and intellectuals and independent women. Grace Ogot's novel, *The Promised Land* conceptualizes the ideal obedient African wife, who is community-oriented with non-materialistic goals. Charles Mangua's fictional autobiographical novel, *Son of a Woman* records the miserable life of a harlot in slums.

Elechi Amadi, a Nigerian educator, novelist and dramatist is concerned with the traditional life and the native system of values in his novels. Amadi's early novels are set in the traditional Africa, a pre-colonial situation in Nigeria. *The Concubine* (1966) depicts the village life, age-old customs and native faith. *The Great Ponds* (1969) is about a war between two villages over fishing rights. His third novel *The Slave* published in 1978 is about enslavement and sufferings of the deprived class of society. *Estrangement* speaks of the after-effects of the civil wars in Nigeria. His first three novels deal with personal and intimae aspects of the lives of his characters rather than the public and larger issues that concern their clan. Amadi's focus is the individual, and the forces—social, psychological, actual and supernatural—influencing his actions, and determines the quality of his existence.

The writings of Kalamu are centred on the task of liberating the larger African-American community from an oppressive, domineering white authority and culture where human beings are exploited and treated like cattle for sale in the market. African society is suffused with black male prerogative, black male dominance and violence. Women are relegated as rural work force to be used in farming for tending animals and nurturing children. Even at the time of community festivals and celebrations and ceremonies, only men actively participate while women are just onlookers from the fringe, like outsiders. For a long time, African women remained neglected, exploited and suppressed. They neither participated in decision-making nor were allowed to speak out their mind on vital issues pertaining their village and clan.

Postcolonial literature presents a wide range of experience in societies with cultural angularities and divergences. Ashcroft, Griffith and Tiffin defined postcolonialism in terms of: migration, slavery, suppression, resilience, representation, difference, race, gender, place and responses to the influential master discourses of imperial Europe.[3]

Colonial rule subjected Africans to utter humiliation, loss of cultural identity and political enslavement and also economic deprivation. In the postcolonial situation after achieving political independence, it has become the primary task of modern African writer to restructure the native society and restore its cultural identity. Chinua Achebe, Wole Soyinka, Ekwensi and others in their own way have endeavored to re-educate and regenerate African society through the re-discovery of the past.

Chinua Achebe, the doyen of modern African writing in English, exhorts Africans not to degrade themselves just because of black colour but to take pride in what is African. About the theme of his writings, he says:

> As far as I am concerned the fundamental theme is that African people did not hear of culture for the first time from Europeans; that their societies were not mindless but frequently had a philosophy of great depth and value and beauty, that they had poetry and, above all, they had dignity. It is this dignity that African people all but lost during the colonial period and it is this that they must now regain.[4]

Chinua Achebe holds that the traditional society in Africa has not given importance to women in community affairs. But Beatrice in *Anthills of the Savannah*, with her Honours Degree from Queen Mary College, University of London, represents 'new' woman with her distinct vision. She is articulate, independent and self-reliant and evaluates women's position by their assertion. It's not enough that women should be the court of the last resort because the last resort is a damn sight too far and too late!

Beatrice affirms moral strength and intellectual integrity of African woman, in the changed postcolonial situation in Nigeria. Urbanization and 'new' education have broadened women's horizon. Ikem, the editor of the National Gazette supports advancement in life and her self-supportive role. Achebe through Beatrice seems to be championing the cause of woman and her progress. Further, in the novel, he exposes the attitude of new rulers in a sovereign state. In the novel Ikem speaks of "leaders who openly looted our treasury, whose effrontery soiled out national soul." And he cautions Nigerians:

> You must develop the habit of skepticism, not to swallow every piece of superstition you are told by witch doctors and professors

> when you read yourself of these things your potentiality for assisting and directing this nation will be quadrupled. [5]

Chinua Achebe's *Anthills of Savannah* and Kole Omotoso's *Just before Dawn* are experimental novels in the last two decades in the sense that Achebe's novel has recorded the decline of human interest when the civilian is overthrown by a military junta and on the other hand Omotoso's work intermingled real historic and fictional element to divulge the shattered picture of the modern Nigeria both in the hands of the British and the politicians eager to grab power after independence.

Wole Soyinka, the Nigerian playwright, poet, novelist and social critic was the first African writer to win the most coveted Nobel Prize for Literature in 1986. Soyinka was cited by the Swedish Academy of Letters as a writer "who in a wide cultural perspective and with poetic overtones, fashions the drama of existence." He studied at the University College of Ibadan, where Chinua Achebe and Christopher Okigbo were his contemporaries and at the Varsity College he was the editor of "The Eagle," a cyclostyled news-sheet of a student political organization. Then he moved to Leeds to work for a degree in drama. Leeds offered him many theatrical productions. Soyinka is known for his quick wit and fertile imagination. For supporting the coup in Nigeria in 1966, he was imprisoned in 1967 and was subsequently released in 1969 as part of 'Independence Anniversary Amnesty'. He revealed his arrest and imprisonment in his memoirs *The Man Died* published in 1972. He was the founding Director of the Orisun Theatre and The 1960 Masks Theatre at Lagos and Ibadan.

Wole Soyinka is a highly cultivated and very practical man, an actor, producer and theatre-administrator. He is a man of considerable independence and moral courage and a critic of his own society. Dealing with the problems of his society, he has exposed the evils and political injustices in his works. Soyinka operates primarily in a satiric mode and sometimes incorporates traditional Yoruba myths and rituals to heighten the satire. He has satirized the new men in power for becoming power crazy and selfish and is incensed with the hypocrisy of religious leaders and the intellectuals for their apathy and ineffectuality. He is critical about the transition in Nigeria.

His *The Road* (1965) is a study in the psychology of transition, the hangover etc. Here the professor, the protagonist, is a frustrated artist who has developed a passionate love for the white man's civilization and has acquired all the trappings only to discover that they do not truly belong to that culture. His another play *The Trials of Brother Jero* is a farce, hilariously funny, exposing the deceit and hypocrisy of a religious leader. *The Lion and the Jewel* is built around a love triangle with two suitors representing tradition and transition trying to win the bride Sidi who represents feminity, some form of goddess of Earth.

In *Kongi's Harvest* also, Segi, the courtesan and ex-mistress of Kongi symbolizes fertility, one aspect of the Earth Mother. Segi is portrayed as a militant, a fit match to challenge the authority of self-styled, power-crazy dictators like Kongi. Soyinka has drawn deeply both from his native Yoruba culture and Christian education to mould the events in Nigeria to reeducate his society like many African writers.

Even though Amos Tutuola is not a sophisticated writer and his works are branded as "ghost novels" and "naïve romances" written in 'Yong English', 'semi-literate English', his first work *The Palm-Wine Drinkard* is really a significant work of fiction in English by a black West African. It is based on Yoruba folk tales, about the adventurous journey of the palm-wine drinkard into the forests to search for his tapster in the country of the dead. The narrative is but a fantastic series of episodes and incredible experiences of the drinkard.

Mongo Beti is another prolific writer whose works trace the history of Africa. Some works are social and political and others deal with familial ties in the new political dispensation. In an interview given to Boniface Mongo-Mboussa, he criticizes the indifferent attitude of bourgeois. He says that they have beautiful houses, they eat well, they run after women, etc. There is a kind of indifference amongst the elite vis-à-vis the poorer members of the population. For alongside the corrupt and carefree elites, there are those who cannot go to hospital because there is no equipment, children who cannot go to school because their parents have no money, girls who go into prostitution because they are hungry, etc. But it absolutely does not trouble this 'bourgeoisie' and he feels very much disappointed.

In his novel *Mission to Kala*, Medza is set off in search of a villager's wife who has run away with a man belonging to another tribe. *The Poor Christ of Bomba* is a true account of betrayal of the local churchmen in the name of religion. They have used local girls prepared for Christian marriage in the women's camp for their own purposes.

Biyi Bandele-Thomas, a Nigerian playwright, poet and novelist writes about institutionalized brutality in his country. He is poetic and satirical when he speaks of the politics of violence, sufferings inflicted by the military, the police and the politicians. His novel The Man Who Came in from the Back of Beyond is a story of Africa-exotic, sprawling, overcrowded and bizarre and it also speaks of the relationship between a student and a literary teacher, a sub-plot in the novel. Maude, a teacher narrates the story of his student's former boyfriend in the first person narration. The novel has presented the deteriorating conditions of life and militarism in modern Nigeria.

Ben Okri's fiction is one of the most significant exploitations of literary form in the canon of postcolonial African literature. Ben Okri's works include five novels and two collections of short stories and a volume of poetry dealing with the themes pertaining to postcolonialism. Rampant corruption and violence in Nigeria are dealt with besides voicing the concerns for the poor and deprived class of the African society.

Ama Ata Aidoo's *Our Sister Killjoy* speaks of the social and economic condition of women in the contemporary society. Sissie's voyage to Europe provides her opportunity to know her status in the past during the colonial period and in the new political dispensation. She tries to assert herself in the changed political order and power hierarchy. As Abena Busia argues, "One of the primary characteristics in the representation of the black African woman in colonial fiction is the construction of her inactive silence."[6]

Even the Bible made women conscious of their existential necessity for the man. The Bible orders women to obey their husbands and submit themselves to them in a respectable way. In the Lord, however, woman is not independent of man, nor is man independent of woman. (*I Corinthians* 11:11)

Christianity preaches equal treatment to woman while Islam has provided special status to woman, though there is much in-subordination of woman to man in patriarchal society. Though the traditional woman represents fertility, one aspect of Earth Mother, in African society, she too suffers, unable to assert herself. It is proverbially said of the status of traditional woman in Africa that wives and oxen have no friends.

Woman is also the symbol of fortune to a man. "If one is rich, one is not successful as long as one lacks a wife."[7] But African woman is conscious of her role as mother, which she considers her fulfillment. "The satiety of pregnant woman is offspring that is motherhood is a woman's fulfillment."[8]

Keith Booker in *African Novel in English* says that Nnu Ego, the protagonist in Buchi Emecheta's *Joys of Motherhood* provides "trenchant description of the role played by the glorification of motherhood. . .in traditional Igbo society."

In African mythology, woman is regarded as the Earth Mother, to Akposso of Togo she is the first creation and the Ibibio of Nigeria believe that the mother-divinity Eka-Abassi is the originator. In African society woman symbolizes creativity. "She is the mother of life." But widow has no significant role in African traditional society. Africans give much importance to marriage and child bearing and traditional woman participates in religious ceremonies. She represents 'Ani' the goddess of Earth in Igbo traditional society and 'Onile'-in Yoruba tribe proclaiming the decisions of the chief deity as its priestess. And thus she controls the social morality in society. She sometimes becomes part of the jury of the village, counsellor and as ceremonial head she performs the rituals of puberty and death, for her supposed knowledge of the spiritual world. As priestess of the chief deity, she punishes men that offend women.

In the contemporary African society, which is primarily egalitarian, African women demand better treatment and social justice as also political rights. Feminist ideology reflects specificities of the race, class and culture. Not confining themselves to their household, women today have advanced educationally and are economically independent. As professionals and administrators, African women have involved themselves in nation-building activities and for their own advancements.

The traumatic effects of colonialism have made Africans become aware of their exploitation—social, political—and their loss of cultural identity. The 'new' education introduced in the colonial period helped Africans to represent their problems to the administration and to protest against the exploitative policies of the government and also to demand for participation in the local administration.

In *Weep Not Child* of James Ngugi, Ngotho sends his son Njoroge to school to learn 'new' education in the colonial period with the hope that his son would strive to get back the lost lands grabbed by the white man and distributed by them by the new laws framed and promulgated by the administration, to the white settlers and black loyalists. Ezeulu in *The Arrow of God* of Achebe sends his son to the white man's school only to know the secrets of his prowess.

In the changed socio-political scenario today and with the growing concepts of modernization and globalization, African women writers are championing the problems of women in general and contesting the discriminatory laws promulgated if any, affecting the interest of African women in particular. Feminist writers like Flora Nwapa, Buchi Emecheta, Ama Ata Aidoo and others, with a deep concern for the suffering of African women have conferred grace and dignity on womanhood and inspired them to advance in all walks of life as individuals and shaping their own destiny. African women writers endeavour to liberate African women from their traditional bondage, and exploitation on the basis of race, gender and class and self-degradation.

NOTES

1. Abiola Irele, *The African Experience in Literature and Ideology*, p. 11.
2. Frank Katherine, "Women without Men: The Feminist Novel in Africa" *African Literature Today*, 15 (1987): pp. 14-34.
3. Ashcroft Bill, Gareth Griffiths and Helen Tiffin, ed. *Postcolonial Studies Reader* (London: Routledge, 1995).
4. An Interview with Chinua Achebe by Robert Serumaga in the Studies of the Transcription Centre in London in February, 1967.
5. Chinua Achebe, *Anthills of Savannah* (London: Heinemann, 1987).
6. Ama Ata Aidoo, *Our Sister Killjoy* (London: Heinemann, 1977).
7. G. Barra, *1,000 Kikuyu Proverbs*, Nairobi, East African Literature Bureau (London: Macmillan, 1960), p. 2.
8. G. Barra, p. 2.

Chapter II

West African Women Writers

The representation of African women in male-authored works reveals the ideological standpoint of the writers that quite explicitly identifies women with tradition and self-denied role of mother. It reveals women and predators who take to the flesh trade for high life and quick money. African women writers of first generation like Grace Ogot, Flora Nwapa have focused on the marginalized position of women and need to revolt against exploitation and oppression of women in African society. But contemporary African women writers deal with a postcolonial reality where both customary and common laws of marriage apply.

African woman writing as a 'multi-voiced discourse' has challenged a number of orthodoxies: 'the voicelessness of the black woman', 'the derogatory portrayals of their gender' and 'their economic marginalization'. West African women writers are concerned with the protest against sex discrimination and woman oppression in patriarchal society. Their writings by presenting the realistic picture of suffering of women appear to have sympathized with the plight of women and denounced their meek submission in male-dominated society.

The chief concerns of most of women writers are polygamy that degraded the status of woman, wife inheritance and her property disinheritance causing a lot of humiliation and ill treatment in her family and society. They have often challenged some of the fundamental assumptions relating to Igbo woman's passively accepting retrogressive cultural norms. By presenting woman as a victim of circumstances created by the society, they seem to have established that woman is not just a commodity to inherit or enjoy but an individual with emotions and desires and ambition and drive in her to advance in life.

In pre-colonial and colonial situation in West Africa, women are pictured as weaker sex, passive, and docile in their traditional role. African patriarchal society has suppressed woman's freedom of expression and economic capabilities. Dr. Rose Ure Mezu, a prominent contemporary writer in Nigeria advocates African female activism. She led the life of a cloistered and protected woman quite ignorant of the problems of women and expected every marriage to resemble like her parents' and every woman to be as loving, strong, reliable and resourceful as her mother.

But she was greatly influenced by Flora Nwapa's Efuru who was placed at the centre of the plot with an ambition to assert her existence as free individual. In a male-oriented society, motherhood and wifehood branded a woman like Nwapa's Efuru 'unfeminine'. And a barren woman as well as a woman with unsuccessful marital life is considered to be useless in her society.

Dr. Rose as the Commissioner in charge of Social Welfare was aware of daily oppressions and marginalisation of Nigerian woman. And her pursuit for Ph.D. brought her into contact with feminist theorists and their perception of the plight of women. She realized that black women are no more considered intellectually inferior to men but their lives largely distorted, deemed to be insignificant.

Florence Nwanzuruahu Nkiru Nwapa is the first West African woman novelist to champion the cause of women in particular in West Africa. She is a prolific Nigerian writer, a feminist depicting the suffering of female in the new political dispensation in Nigeria. Born on January 18, 1931 in Oguta, East Central State, Nigeria, she is the first African woman to publish in English. She obtained a degree from University College, Ibadan in 1957. Later, she did a diploma in education from the University of Edinburgh and also worked for one year as Educational Officer in the Ministry of Education in Clabar.

Her love for teaching took her to Queen's School in Enugu where she taught English and geography for three years. She also held various administrative positions such as Assistant Registrar, University of Lagos; Minister of Health and Social welfare, East Central State; and Minister of Lands, Survey and Urban Development. But she continued her life mostly as an educator teaching at colleges and universities including New York University, Trinity College, University of Minnesota, University of Michigan and University of Illorin.

Flora Nwapa became a popular writer for depicting Igbo life and customs from a woman's point of view. She is acknowledged as the first internationally acclaimed woman novelist of black Africa written in the English language. She is called the mother of Modern African literature. She is awarded by her own town Oguta, the highest chieftaincy title 'Ogbuefi' which is an achievement award given to men. She has written many stories compiled into volumes meant for children with Nigerian setting and with profound message. Besides her being a writer and teacher, she has also become an entrepreneur setting her own example to others contrary to the traditional roles of women. Though she never likes to be called a feminist, her writings deal with feminism, the cause of woman.

She has openly confessed in an interview with Marie Umeh that women are more independent and industrious. "When I do write about women in Nigeria, in Africa, I try to paint a positive picture about women because there are many women who are very, very positive, in their thinking, who are very, very independent, and very, very industrious."[1]

Flora Nwapa's first two novels *Efuru* and *Idu*, published in 1966 and 1971, carried name for her as a writer to reckon with. Distressed with the attitude of her publisher Heinemann Education, she determined to establish Tana Press Limited in 1977 to publish her other works and the works of her other contemporary writers. The women in her novels are impressive in their roles as promoters of African cultural traditions and protectors of cultural heritage. They often use prayers, lullabies, proverbs, riddles, folk songs and tales, mainly to protect African character and shape African personality.

Her novels have also drawn from oral literature material for her characterization and dramatization of situation. Sometimes for her lengthy dialogues, she appears to be rhetorical. She has always asserted and highlighted the feminine principle, the prime cultural factor in African life to make women become conscious of herself and her individual creativity. She has stressed that the institution of marriage should never act as a barrier to female-actualization. Her feminine perspective shows that female characters not only accelerate the actions of men around but also shape their destiny.

The world of Flora Nwapa's first two novels—*Efuru* and *Idu*—reflects patriarchy. It is a world bounded on a value system that is conducive to man's pleasure and self-realization. Women have no option to assert themselves but to obey and follow the dictates of their husbands. And a woman's life is significant as long as the prestige of the man and the integrity of the family are intact.

In *Efuru* woman is portrayed merely as a sex object to satisfy man's desire and taste. Efuru is subjected to clitoridectomy 'by having a bath' in contrast to circumcision in man, only to denigrate woman, to make her potentially weak. The 'bath' is used as a metaphor to show that woman is inferior to man, biologically speaking.

As a pious lady upholding the divine principles of Ugwuta Community, Nwapa notes that women priestesses are the privileged class and are revered in their society. The sacrificing nature of women, in Nwapa's novels, reflects the importance of priesthood to be treated on par with men in the patriarchal society in Nigeria. She confers dignity and identity on African woman in an attempt to establish female literary tradition with realistic approach. She has never troubled her heroines especially when they are central to the main plot by dint of their hard work and honesty.

Nwapa unleashed a new tradition in African letters making one-dimensional, monotonous depiction of women triumph as femme fatales. Female bonding to Flora Nwapa is female solidarity. Her views on the institution of marriage and familial relationship that she proclaimed at the Second International Feminist Book Fair in Oslo, Norway, are noteworthy: "If we as women pay less attention to men and marriage. . . . I am married and I have children. But I don't live for my husband alone. I live for him, for my children and for my profession."[2]

Her creative works abound in the use of colloquial Igbo proverbs that are didactic and have identified women as carriers of Ugwuta verbal art. She never remained content with her publication of adult novels but she also went on to scribble children's books, and wrote plays and essays. She exhibited her books at International Conferences and Book Fairs to expose her women-centred perspective to academics and masses all over the globe. Her Tana Press remained instrumental in the circulation of her books throughout Africa, Europe, Asia and the United States of America. Her books enabled the scholars and students of African literature studies to become inquisitive to probe further into even her unpublished works.

Toni Morrison, the first African-American woman to receive the Nobel Prize for Literature in 1993, in an interview on her essay, "Rootedness: The Ancestor as Foundation," implores the people to ruminate the great ancestor: "If you kill the ancestor you will kill yourself. Let us continue to keep Flora Nwapa, our ancestor, alive by disseminating for ideas and her philosophy with the same energy that her own artistic life radiated."[3]

Nwapa's lucid, thought provoking and spiritually charged writing is an endeavour to differentiate herself intellectually from other literary writers. She carved a niche for herself in her works by merging gender based relationship controversy with that of national discourse. Nwapa, a skilful manipulator of language, employs lucid language mainly to stimulate a serious situation involving social and moral issues that are faced by the Igbo woman in her daily activities.

Flora Nwapa's plots appear to be simple, woven with complex symbolism, comic interventions and skilful dialogues with sprinkled anecdotes and moral judgements. She reinforces the notion that a woman can change her mind based on situation and thus she does not necessarily bring peace and respect to her people. She focuses on the unsympathetic husbands harassing their barren wives. On the other hand, she proves how fast a tender-hearted man succumbs to female seduction and changes his habits when he loses control over his life. In *One is Enough*, Amaka's husband Obiora who often beats her suddenly becomes submissive when Amaka, a passive recipient, turns ferocious and knocks him down assuming the opposite role.

Like Efuru, Nwapa too is an illustrious successful woman shaping her own destiny. She, as the mystery of Uhamiri exemplifying female authority, has influenced her society in her own way, in particular women. She prepares her audience to accept and approve the sufferings of her protagonists in her two novels *Efuru* and *Idu*, and also *Never Again* to become successful in life. In each of her novels, Nwapa tries to diagnose the maladies of her characters, and community and suggests certain precautionary measures to overcome her difficulties and suffering.

The most distressing of all kinds of maladies is childlessness, lamenting the lack of fertility among Nigerian women. Nwapa considers woman not just a vessel, empty or filled, but also a decision-making personality. She revolts against such humiliation women are subjected to as weak and meek persons unable to raise their voice. Nwapa as mother and teacher recites a tale in the African oral tradition to the African women consoling and cautioning them and also expects them to respond to her call.

Her last two novels—*One is Enough* and *Women Are Different*—reached Nigerians as clarion calls to redefine their lives. She makes a fictive exploration of child figures by projecting them onto the canvas of childhood, thereby creating a conscious symbolism to revise the patriarchal norms in the society. Nwapa quite often with skilful craftsmanship returns to the religious fantasy with Uhamiri as source emphasizing the idea that there exists no hierarchy in terms of gender between the gods and goddesses for the acquisition of more power.

Nwapa is greatly influenced by the works of Chinua Achebe, Ernest Hemingway and Charles Dickens. The symbol of crossroads dominates literary production. She herself faced many challenges in the world. She stabilizes her position through economic independence and self-reliance. She identifies herself with African women who are shrewd market women, energetic female cultivators and rebellious wives and also the sacrificial mothers.

Nwapa never likes to be addressed as feminist though her works question African tradition and plead for reformation of women. She has skilfully synthesized the traditional Igbo mores and myths with imported views of women for the creation of complex characters yearning for independence. Nwapa is convinced that in African tradition, a woman enjoys the privilege of breaking and sharing a kola if only her industry and accomplishments are estimated. She concludes that sexism stands as the second problem emerging out of race, class and the exploitation of people of colour.

Flora Nwapa's Efuru is a living model of a woman craving to become mother. She approaches Uhamiri, the goddess of Ogbuide, for fertility. She silently suffers humiliation in the society, and when she gives birth to a child she feels as if she has conquered the whole world. She loves her child more than herself and when her husband Adizua fails to attend the funeral, as an affectionate mother she divorces Adizua and blames him for lack of concern for her child and much against the tradition, goes for a second marriage: "Efuru came back after a month and vowed that it was over with her and Adizua. She told herself that even if Adizua came back and begged her on his knees with a bag of money, she would not listen to him."[4] Efuru openly declares to her mother-in-law that she can't live with her husband anymore.

> I cannot wait indefinitely for Adizua, you can bear witness that I have tried my best. I am still young and wish to marry again. It will be unfair both to you and your son if I begin to encourage men who would like to marry me while still in the house. (*Ibid*)

Idu in Flora Nwapa's *Idu* is the most affectionate and selfless wife of Adiewere. She is disappointed as she could not conceive and consoles herself by encouraging her husband to marry a second time. But after some time, when she conceives, she dreams of her happy life with her husband in a newly constructed house.

When Adiewere thinks of divorcing his second wife, Idu prevents him from taking such a drastic step. Adiewere suddenly vomits and dies in the bathroom and Idu, after delivering a child, dies after a few days. She proves that she not only craved to become a mother but also remained loyal to her husband and concerned about his happiness.

African woman is also viewed as an object of sex meant for physical gratification. For most of the women writers in Africa, this attitude towards women has formed the basis for feminism. Flora Nwapa's Amaka in her *One is Enough* is portrayed as an object of sex. She is deeply hurt when she comes to know that her husband has illicit relations with another woman. She is helpless and forced to tolerate her suffering. Moreover her mother-in-law also approves her son's having a second wife who has children. Amaka could not restrain herself long and picks a quarrel with her husband Obiora:

> You have changed a good deal, my husband, I too could change you know. Meaning what? Meaning that I could do a lot behind your back without ever finding out, she said. Like prostitution? No, God forbid our land forbids that. What would you do behind my back? Nothing, Nothing? Yes, Nothing, I won't be a prostitute, that's all I know. What then? Sleep around with other men? Out with it. What would you do behind my back? I am not a man. I am a woman.[5]

She becomes conscious of her self-identity in her definition of herself as a wife, a slave to tradition. "As a wife I am never free. I am a shadow of myself." (*Ibid.*, 127)

Nwapa's son Uzoma Nwakuche considers her only as a mother rather than a woman with various roles including and that of writer but his assessment proves wrong. Nwapa first suffered from arthritis and then pneumonia and breathed her last in October 1993 at the age of 62. She was buried at Amede's Court in Scarsdale, New York. The doyen of African female writers has left an indelible impression on the minds of Africans in general and the readers of African Literature and Studies in particular.

Buchi Emecheta, another successful writer with astounding academic record, began her university career at the age of twenty-two. Born on July 21, 1944 in Yaba near Lagos, Nigeria, she was orphaned in her early childhood and had early education at a missionary school. After the death of her parents, she remained neglected by her relatives. Her traumatic experience and suffering at an early age turned her into a feminist.

In 1960, at the age of 16, she got married to Sylvester Onwordi, a student with whom she had been in love since she was eleven. They moved to London, thereby fulfilling the desire of her dead father that at least a member from their family should go to London. And after six years of her marriage, she was blessed with five children. She struggled hard to sustain her family and faced many hardships in life. She assumed several roles such as mother, student, worker and writer. She translated her works into fourteen languages. When she was asked about her literary works, she replied: "If I was not to perish here, I realized that I find something I was good at. My books are about survival, just like my own life."[6] She mostly wrote for her children and she modestly remarked that her writings lacked creativity.

> Well, I admit that I am not really very creative. I have to experience something or know someone who has seen something in order to write convincingly. People keep on going back to them because when they read them they see a mirror of their own lives. (*Ibid.*)

After obtaining her degree in Sociology, Buchi Emecheta took to writing. Her Nigerian compatriot Flora Nwapa immensely influenced her and she calls herself Nwapa's sister. She is lively, energetic and a strong woman unaffected even by her own success. The problems and prejudices of black people and especially degradation and humiliation of Black women are subjects of her writings.

She has drawn material from her own life to focus the problems of black immigrant women. She has a dual role to perform as writer and social worker. She has produced thirteen novels, three autobiographical works and four children's books and also has written plays for the BBC. She is conscious of her roots in Africa.

And she has presented women in different roles in both the traditional and immigrant societies. Like Achebe she too is greatly concerned about the Igbo culture. To her Igbo is an emotional tongue full of proverbs and sayings reflecting ancestral wisdom. She is conscious of black woman's awareness of racial and gender discrimination. Some of African male writers consider her to be a hostile immigrant with prejudiced European views.

Emecheta has analyzed African women only from her point of view. Her works deal with the social norms of African culture such as polygamy, son-preference and wife inheritance. She depicts the life of woman with a sense of commitment to focus gender and class relations, cutting across racial and geographical boundaries.

Buchi Emecheta writes in her works how women, when displaced from the rural setting, move to urban areas where gender system is flexible and almost non-existent and enjoy certain amount of freedom and autonomy. Women often find themselves in disadvantageous position compared to men. Emecheta and Mariama Ba illustrate how a woman who is a senior wife has at least three things that stand in her favour, which she can use with impunity—her position of senior wife; her status as mother; and her status as the mother of her sons since her sons are the direct heirs to the property of family.

Buchi Emecheta uses the strong oral traditions of Africa to represent aspects and values of native culture. She believes in the writer being an oral communicator: "I believe it is important to speak to the readers in person . . . to enable people to have a whole picture of me; I have to both write and speak. I view my role as a writer and also as oral communicator." (*Ibid.*)

The Joys of Motherhood, one of Buchi Emecheta's finest novels, could not impress the readers in Nigeria when the country was undergoing a great political and economic change. The main character Nnuego defines the validity of her womanhood solely by the success of her children. Her fulfillment is centred on her desire to uphold motherhood, and to see her children happy and prosperous. But she faces many disappointments and finds her grown-up children unhappy. For her own misfortune and other disasters, she considers herself responsible.

In agony and physical suffering of Nnuego, Emecheta symbolizes gender suppression in African society. Nnuego's happy and carefree life ends in her marriage and after that she starts living a docile life in the company of her children. She supports her husband in his business but the earnings are insufficient to sustain the family. And even the happiness of her motherhood remains a myth. For her the joy of being a mother is a joy of giving all to her children. Nnuego realizes that money and family progress do not go together.

> She had reminded herself of the old saying that money and children don't go together: if you spent all your time making money and getting rich, the gods wouldn't give you any children; if you wanted children, you had to forget money, and be content to be poor. Nnuego realized that part of the pride of was to lock a little unfashionable and be able to draw with joy: 'I can't afford another outfit because I'm nursing him, so you see I can't go anywhere to sell anything.'[7]

Buchi Emecheta has been criticized for presenting "stereotypic portrayals of African women" with emphasis only on gender and not any other serious activity involving her woman protagonist. Her main concerns centre on the "biological and marital aspects of women's lives central to which are motherhood, bride wealth and polygamy." She uses the theme of motherhood with a view to reconstructing women's gender identity, to move beyond gender as sexual difference. The exchange of women, marriage, child bearing, child rearing are the various social issues, she tries to highlight to show the male-female relationship grounded in the male-oriented society. Though she has championed the cause of woman, she refuses to be called a feminist. But she has admitted that her works advocate liberation of women, and has claimed that she is just a womanist. And she has succeeded in realizing her dreams.

Akosua Busia, born in Ghana, belongs to a new generation of African women writers from outside Africa. Like Buchi Emecheta, she too left her homeland and returned only for brief spells. She was educated at Oxford University and settled in Los Angeles. She contributed to the screenplay of Jonathan Demme's film adoption of Toni Morrison's *Beloved*, and acted in films, such as Low Blow (1986), Native Son (1987) and Brother Future (1991). Her first novel *The Seasons of Been to Black Bird* (1996) reveals the condition of African Diaspora in the context of post-colonial situation.

Ama Ata Aidoo, a rebellious writer of Africa held various positions such as Consulting Professor to the Phelps-Strokes Funds in Washington during 1974 and 1975. She compiled eleven short stories in a volume entitled *No Sweetness Here* revealing the impact of the conquest on Africa in the economic and cultural spheres. She published her poems while studying at the University of Ghana in 1964. She was privileged to work with Efua Sutherland, founder of the Ghana Drama Studio. She wrote stories only to bring about change among women. She believed that the man of Africa alone wasn't able to advance without establishing relationship with the West and the rest of the world.

The Dilemma of a Ghost, a play published in 1965, brought her name and fame as a dramatist. The play is concerned with the problem of conflict between traditional culture and western education and values. In 1977 she succeeded in publishing her full-length novel *Our Sister Killjoy*, a work of art. This novel depicts the impact of African encounter with Europe on African people in general and women in particular. Her craftsmanship lies in her linking concerns of women with social issues.

In 1982, she was appointed Minister for Education in the military regime in Ghana for 18 months. Later on Aidoo shifted to Zimbabwe where she concentrated on both curriculum development unit of the Ministry of Education and Zimbabwe women writers. Besides being a novelist and short story writer, she has also published her first collection of poetry, *Some One Talking Some Time*. Like Buchi Emecheta, she also wrote for children. *Changes: A Love Story*, her second novel, also became popular in Ghana.

Changes won Commonwealth Writers Prize for the best book for the African region and brought her recognition. Aidoo reasserted her theme of woman's position as economic, social, political being in the contemporary African society. Her financial independence encouraged her to examine and question the values of her own culture. She rhetorically poses many questions as to why women are not treated on par with men. Her protest is explicit in the following heart-felt cry.

> Why had they sent her to school?
> What had they hoped to gain from it?
> What had they hoped she would gain from it?
> Who had designed the educational system that had produced her sort?
> What had that person or persons hoped to gain from it?[8]

Aidoo has defined the word nationalism used by the new rulers as an instrument meant to suppress the aspirations of people. She mocked at the educated Africans who called themselves real patriots but who are lured by the material advancement. She projects Africa with its distinct identity from a female perspective.

> "My dear young man," said the visiting professor, "to give you the decent answer your anxiety demands, I would have to tell you a detailed history of the African continent and to do that, I shall have to speak every day, twenty-four hours a day, for at least three thousand years. And I don't mean to be rude to you or anything, but who has that kind of time?"[9]

Ama Ata Aidoo hailing from Ghana and Emecheta from Nigeria have much in common. Emecheta as a divorcee lived with her four children; Aidoo a few years older to Emecheta was a widow and lived with her only daughter. Both are African women writers known also outside Africa and lived in exile—Emecheta in London and Aidoo in Zimbabwe. Emecheta's exile is personal and professional while Aidoo's is overtly political. Because of male domination, Emecheta could publish only a dozen works including her own autobiography and stories for children.

Aidoo, a playwright, poet, novelist, radical socialist, Ghanaian leader and an outspoken woman, faced bitter criticism from her own people. Both the writers enthusiastically delivered lectures at the universities in the United States and Britain. Both experienced denigration in their society partly because of their traditional customs and practices. Aidoo's *Changes* and Emecheta's *Kehinde* are similar in their recording of woman's experience.

Esi divorces Oko and marries Ali Kondey only to find that in the polygamous society, second marriage would never end in happiness. Similarly Kehinde divorces Albert and marries her Caribbean lover but she too repents. Ama Ata Aidoo mixes European realism with choral communalism, to record her universal experience of woman. Emecheta's domestic realism clashes with self-consciousness in dealing with a similar theme. Kehinde and Esi are middle-class women and educated entrepreneurs earning more than their husbands. Both are independent, owning their houses but losing their children to their husbands. Both find solace in female friendship. Both had bitter experience in life with lecherous male—Esi with her friend's husband and Kehinde with the hotel housekeeper.

Between the two authors, Emecheta is a less explicit feminist. In her essay "Feminism with a small 'f'" in *Criticism and Ideology*, a volume of papers of the 1986 Second African Writers Conference in Stockholm (Scandinavian Institute of African Studies, 1988) she discusses woman's problems from African woman's point of view:

> Being a woman and African born, I see things through an African woman's eyes. . . . I did not know that by doing so I was going to be called a feminist. But if I am now a feminist that I am an African feminist with a small 'f' . . . I write about women who try very hard to hold their family together until it becomes absolutely impossible.[10]

Aidoo feels that feminism is something that has been imported into Africa to strain the cordial relationship between African women and African men.

The Black women writers of 1970s and 1980s have emphasized the black feminist thought exploring the aspects of black feminism. Alice Walker's novel *In Search of Our Mother's Gardens* (1983) and Barbara Smith's *Anthology of Black Women's Writings* (1983) have dealt with the issues relating to black lesbianism. Filomina Chioma Steady's essay on *African Feminism: A Worldwide Perspective* (1987) has traced the development of black feminist thought inside and outside Africa especially among the intellectual class. Contemporary black feminism has spread itself in multiple organizational setting.

Black women earlier represented their grievances to the traditional organizations such as churches, clubs and local organizations. Later new black women's organizations like professional associations were formed to champion their cause. Black feminist intellectual's writings as pieces of propaganda also helped in spreading black feminism, meant to bring awareness among especially the black women. The black feminist popular agenda has been to make African woman acquire leadership qualities to advance in life. Thus feminism emerged also as a political movement, promoting black feminist thought, and to forge black women with their distinct vision into future as an intellectual force.

Though African-American women disagreed on the agenda and the concept of black feminism, it attracted many blacks all over the world in general and the black in Africa in particular. The early black feminists are responsible for the emergence of black feminism as a rigorous and progressive movement in America.

Toni Morrison, the first black woman to be awarded the Nobel Prize for Literature in 1993, believes in the dynamic spirit of community reflected in folklore, mythology and native culture. After graduation, she entered Howard University, secured a degree in English and Classics and enrolled herself in a graduate school at Cornel University where she worked on the works of Virginia Woolf and William Faulkner for her Master's thesis. She served as English Instructor at Texas Southern University, Howard University, and State University of New York at Albany and at Princeton. She married Harold Morrison, a Jamaican architect but got separated in 1964 and moved to Syracuse, New York, to become editor for Random House.

Her first novel The Bluest Eye was published in 1970. Her literary career is marked by many honours such as National Book Critics Award, Pulitzer Prize, and Robert F. Kennedy Award. In her novels she has focused the experiences of Black Americans in particular the Black Women, the deprived section of the so-called civilized society. She has also discussed in her works racial, class and gender problems of women. Like Flora Nwapa, Toni Morrison highlights black woman's oppression in male-dominated society and her craving for cultural identity. She uses fantasy and native myths and folklore for authenticity.

Her magazine *Salone* revealed her vision into future of black women as individuals and responsible citizens of their nation. Her novels are an enquiry to better the condition of woman and for projecting a promising image of black woman in her native country. She has declared in her lecture at Princeton that she wants to write for people like her, which is to say black people, curious people, demanding people—people who can't be faked, people who don't need to be patronized, people who have very, very high criteria.

In an interview with Jean Strouse, Morrison has revealed how her childhood experiences influenced her works. She has said that those were not written for a little black girl in Lorain, Ohio, but they were so magnificently done that she got them anyway and they spoke directly to her out of their own specificity.

The potentiality of black South African is revealed in a short lyric.

> You have touched the women,
> You have struck a rock,
> You have dislodged a boulder,
> You will be crushed.[11]

African women writers as spokeswomen of African women going into the history of feminist politics, woman's rights and her suppression and deprivation have focused on the predicament of women in America and Africa. In feminist issues in the fiction of Kenya's women writers, O'Barr classifies feminist concerns into three main categories: "How female children become women . . . what marriage means for women . . . where women's work fits into their lives." She has also admitted: "All I write is from the women's point of sharply underscoring the idea that the female perspective may be different from the male perspective on the same topic."[12]

About the significant roles of Kenyan women, she said: "They see themselves performing traditional roles . . . without traditional resources . . . while at the same time they are under-taking modern activities . . . while being denied access to modern support systems." (*Ibid.*)

Katherine Frank in her controversial article, *Women without Men, the Feminist Novel in Africa* tries to influence African women with her radically feminist thought. Kofi Owusu emphasizes on Aidoo's linguistic, textual manipulations and the complex image of women in African literature. Elleke Boehmer highlights the portrayal of women as mothers, whores, symbols of national pride, spiritual advisers, and builders of nation but not as individuals actively involved in political activity.

In Achebe's *Anthills of the Savannah*, Boehmer criticizes Achebe's attempts to include women in his renovation of the past and present women merely as a vehicle of transformation rather than as individuals with active role in the nation-building activities. For her, "Woman is a ground of change or discursive displacement but not the subject of transformation." (*Ibid.*)

Mariama Ba, a native of Senegal, was brought up by her grandparents in a traditional environment. Her father was active in politics and became a Minister for Health. She secured a diploma in teaching in 1947 and remained in the teaching profession for twelve long years. Owing to ill health, she gave up teaching and got married to a Member of Parliament, Obeye Diop. In 1980, she was awarded Noma prize for her first novel *So Long a Letter*. But she died the following year before the publication of her second novel, *Scarlet Song*.

In her novel *So Long a Letter*, she followed the norm of epistolary art. She dealt with the problems like polygamy, caste system and exploitation confronting woman even in the civilized society. Ramatoulaya who later becomes a widow records her poignant endurance when her husband decides to marry Binetou. The novel *Scarlet Song* portrays the failure of the marriage of a young Senegalese man with a young French woman. The desecration of the institution of marriage and the pertinent factors like family opposition, husband's weakness of character and the cultural shock of expatriate spouse that disrupt inter-racial marriages are vividly portrayed in the novel.

Mariama Ba upholds women's struggle for liberation and independent existence and their rightful place in literature. As women we must work for our own future, we must overthrow the statuesque which harms us and we must no longer submit to it like men, we must use literature as non-violent but as an effective weapon. We no longer accept the nostalgic praise to the African mother who, in his anxiety man confuses with mother Africa. Women have a place within African literature, the place due to them on the basis of their participation side by side—with men—in all places of the liberation struggle and their contribution to economic development but women will have to fight for the place with all their might.[13]

Nadine Gordimer, a South African woman novelist born in 1923 in a well-to-do family in the small mining town of springs outside Johannesburg, South Africa, is concerned about the moral and psychological tensions in her racially divided home country besides the depiction of master-servant relations, spiritual and sexual paranoia of colonialism and the shallow liberalism of her privileged white compatriots. She has personally experienced the impact of the treatment given to the black majority by the minority whites. She was a founding member of Congress of South African Writers and was awarded Nobel Prize for Literature in 1991.

Gordimer did not write an autobiography, as she is too jealous of her privacy and did not want to reveal herself in her works. She vehemently opposed Apartheid, a policy of racial segregation, for nearly half a century. As a keen observer, she has recorded even minute details of human relationship in her works. The novel *Living Days* is about Helen, a white girl, and her growing dissatisfaction and dislike towards the parochial attitude of people in a small town.

Her new novel, *The House Gun* set in contemporary post-apartheid South Africa, speaks of immorality. The book is about a privileged couple whose life becomes topsy-turvy when their son is accused of murder. When they rush to a talented black lawyer for help, they become too sentimental and become conscious of their genuine problem.

Bessie Head, born in South Africa in 1937 to a Scottish mother and Black South African father, was brought up in a foster home. She attended a missionary school and later graduated herself to become a teacher. After moving to Botswana, she started living in constant fear that the government might deport her back to South Africa. Her mother's psychic problems too distressed her much. This has a direct bearing on her works but one can see a note of hope and optimism underlying it.

Charlotte Bruner, a professor of Literature at the University of Iowa, and African editor of the *Feminist Companion to English Literature*, produced a weekly radio series *First Person Feminine* for over six years in the United States. Her popular anthology *Unwinding Threads* contains stories and extracts from novels by women all over Africa. National pride for West African independence, South African voices against political and economic repression and racism, North African women lifting their veils to emerge from enforced domesticity and female servitude are some of her concerns. Though the experience, goals, language, expression and audience differ from one writer to another, yet all their works affirm, as Doris Lessing puts it: "that filter which is a woman's way of looking at life has the same validity as that filter which is a man's way." Calixthe Beyala, a Cameroonian now living in Paris published four novels in France, is considered one of the most promising young writers today. The themes of her novels are Africa and struggle for women's liberation.

African women writers are endowed with a special sensitivity and empathy necessary to creativity. Dr. James in the course of an interview quotes the concerns of the African women writers. It is discovered that women writers have been no less concerned than men to articulate and denounce the poverty, corruption and destructive practices that have impeded development in Africa. At the same time women writers appear to treat more intimately the themes of love and death, transcendence and the struggle to rise above the traditional limitations responsible for women's underdevelopment and oppression.

NOTES

1. An Interview with Flora Nwapa: *The Poetics of Economic Independence for Female Empowerment:* by Marie Umeh, *Research in African Literatures* 26, 2, Summer 1995.
2. Flora Nwapa's paper at the Second International Feminist Book Fair in Oslo, Norway.
3. Toni Morrison, *Rootedness: The Ancestor as Foundation*—An Interview Essay.
4. Flora Nwapa, *Efuru* (London: Heinemann, 1966), 108.
5. Flora Nwapa, *One is Enough* (Enugu: Tana, 1981).
6. Buchi Emecheta's Interview by Julie Holmes in *The Voice*, July 9, 1996.
7. Buchi Emecheta, *The Joys of Motherhood* (London: Heinemann, 1979), 430.
8. Ama Ata. Aidoo, *Changes-A Love Story* (London: Women's Press, 1991).
9. Ama Ata Aidoo, *Our Sister Killjoy* (London: Longman, 1979).
10. Buchi Emecheta, "Feminism with Small 'f'," *Criticism and Ideology*: ed. Kirsten Petersen and Perwestberg (Uppsala: Scandinavian Institute of African Studies, 1988).
11. *African Women's Rights*, A Historical Documentary, South Africa, ed. 1950.
12. Sharon Verba, *Feminist and Womanist Criticism of African Literature: A Bibliography*, July 20, 1997.
13. Ali Mazrui, "The Black Woman and the Problem of Gender: An African Perspective," *Research in African Literature*, Spring, 1993, Volume XXIV No. 1.

Chapter III

The Image of Woman in African Novel

The 'image' is an intellectual and emotional complex at an instant of time. Each individual is identified with a proper name in the society. E. Cassierer calls it the myth-making consciousness.

The African novel presents different images of women in the contemporary patriarchal society. The famous African writers Flora Nwapa, Buchi Emecheta, Ulasi, Chinua Achebe, Wole Soyinka, Cyprian Ekwensi, Amos Tutuola and Ben Okri use African imagery in portraying and dramatizing the characters and situation, for effect and authenticity.

African societies are primarily viewed as masculine. Feminine perspective of Africa and African society, especially about the role of women in African novels, is richly illuminating. In African native religion and African life, it is the image of the chief deity, the goddess of Earth that dominates. The chief deities of the Ewe community of Ghana are Mawu and Lisa. Mawu representing the moon is a female while Lisa symbolizing sun is masculine. The image of Mawu greatly influences the life and living of the people. Though men do not duly regard woman, she is universally acknowledged as the mother of mankind.

Wilfred Cartey's *Whispers from a Continent* places African women geographically in the village. Woman is used as a metaphor of stability. He quotes from Camara Laye's *The Dark Child*: "The nourishing milk comes not only from the natural mother but also from the earth of Africa, mother and earth cross-fertilize and link together to from a single symbol."[1]

Mother Africa is presented in the image of purity, fertility and sustainer of the clan. Africa also assumes negative image in the metaphor originating from the Greco-Roman word standing for chaos, darkness and lack of order. Gender discrimination, family constraints and social restrictions on women are the greatest banes of African society. Some female voices scream that the real place of woman is in her home. However, women are sometimes glorified in their personal life as family caretakers and teachers. Woman constitutes a force to nourish and shapes the young minds in her family. In the tradition-bound society, she is confined to her home discharging her primary duties. The creation of myth and literary image of Africa meaning one's physical attachment, formulates the woman's place in the house.

Women in the superstitious society are the incarnation of supernatural powers. Woman, in most African societies, represents some aspect of the Earth goddess. The Akan of Ghana and the Igbo of Nigeria call the goddess of Earth, Earth Mother. Oya, the goddess of Niger River, one of the wives of Shango, the god of thunder, identifies herself with the wind that blows across the country when no rain falls. In Ghana, special convents are established to train women to become the priestesses of Akonedi shrine.

Marion Kilson opines that wherever goddesses occur, the principal attendants and participants are women. Moreover the rituals are symbolic of essential cultural aspects of womanhood. Dipo of the Krobo and the Bragoro of the Asante in Ghana are worshipped for fertility.

Women, with their intimate knowledge and experience of the spiritual world, as priestesses perform the rituals at the shrine of the goddess of Earth and help in maintaining social morality. Flora Nwapa, the most sought-after feminist, has the Lake Goddess as her guiding principle and tries to bring people closer to the deity even in the changed society. Goddess by virtue of her service becomes part of the society. Nwapa's feminine perspective through the actions of her female characters catalyzes the events in her novels. Lake Goddess Ogbuide, who becomes the kind and powerful mother of Ugwuta community, asserts the feminine principle.

Umuofia the village in *Things Fall Apart* respects only one woman called Chielo, the priestess of the Oracle of the Hills and the Caves. Chielo has a dual role to play—as an ordinary woman and as one to reprimand the offenders of the community. She, as the spokesperson of the deity, screams at Okonkwo when he accompanies his wife and daughter to the shrine of the Oracle of the Hills and the Caves: "Beware of exchanging words with Agbala. Does a man speak when a God speaks? Beware!"[2] Okonkwo, the great warrior and matchless wrestler, rants at Nwoye's mother. "Do what you are told woman. When did you become one of the nidche?" (18) Okonkwo's wife becomes meek and dumb before Chielo.

Nwapa carved a niche for the feminine in her novels. She calls Uhamiri, the female deity of water, the woman of the lake or Mammy Wata. She contrasts Uhamiri with Urashi the male river God only to highlight Uhamiri's innate potential. But Nwapa has portrayed female spirits only to show that they are not subordinates to male spirits as reflected in the dialogue between Urashi and Mammy Wata:

> "You have come at last, Great Spirit of the Lake. It does not to pay to be stubborn, Great Spirit of the lake."
>
> "We have a guest here, Great Spirit of the river. Today is not for quarrel, Great Spirit of the river," replies Mammy Water.
>
> "You always want to quarrel, you proud spirit of the lake," Urashi continues.

Mammy Wata is regarded as one of the wildest spiritual forces, cruel to human beings. However, she is an afflicter and healer, she brings both fortune and misfortune. She is also responsible for infertility, venereal disease and other physical ailments. People worship her for children. The two colours mostly associated with her devotees in West Africa symbolize the deity. Her worshippers wear red and white clothes as a mark of her destruction and creativity. For the Igbo, the red connotes death, danger, power, evil and maleness. Redness is also thought in terms of heat, sacrifice and defilement whereas white colour denotes creativity, peace and birth.

The absence and disgrace of Mammy Wata is believed to create problems not only for women but also for the entire society. Uhamiri who is childless stands as a hope to bless other women with motherhood. Nwapa reminds us that Uhamiri claims a domain to relieve herself from the geopolitical dislocations. Nwapa describes Uhamiri, as an elegant woman, very beautiful combing her long black hair with a golden comb.[3]

She focuses on the fairness of her skin, fine texture of her hair, serenity of her expressions and by the wealth displayed on her person she is akin to Greek gods. She looks odd as she represents the wild spiritual forces and is inconsiderate to human beings. But she is more concerned with the health and prosperity of her followers. Though intellectuals blame Mammy Wata for women's barrenness, venereal diseases, headache and physical distress, others have implicit faith in the goddess who would bestow on them beauty and wealth. She has also cautioned people about misfortunes caused by fortunes showered on them.

Nwapa speaks of the divine machinery at work in the lives of Ugwuta community. Uhamiri, the goddess of the lake, is the most revered in her village whereas in Chinua Achebe's *Things Fall Apart*, Chielo, the Priestess of Agbala, is not regarded always in her village. Ani is worshipped only during the period of New Yam Festival. The people are afraid of Chielo's curse that befalls on the entire community if they go wrong, while Uhamiri is worshipped also for motherhood. Uhamiri is believed to make barren women conceive with her blessings.

Although certain women representing deities are endowed with mystical powers and enjoy special status in their community, ordinary woman fails to command respect in the patriarchal society. She is the most neglected, exploited and degenerated person. Women generally do not actively participate in the meetings of their community. They have no say in decision-making. African woman thus symbolizes passivity and victimization of societal prohibitions as well as certain self-imposed inhibitions.

Ellke Boehmer analyzing, the status of women as mothers, whores, girl friends, wives, free women, courtesans, political women and workers symbolizing national pride and also as spiritual advisers supporting their community, has observed that they have not been presented as individuals actively and respectfully involved in the political activity.

The relationship with a girlfriend is based on mutual love affair and pleasure derived in each other's company whereas the good time girls' relationship is primarily materialistic. Gloria in Aluko's *Chief the Honorable Minister* represents girlfriends symbolizing power and complexity. Gloria is a benevolent and lovable character nursing her lover Moses. She enjoys her status not depending on others.

In *No Longer at Ease* Clara is a nurse but she does not have other responsibilities. Even her relation with Obi Okonkwo would complicate the affairs of Obi's family since Obi's parents do not consent for their marriage. Clara never magnifies the problems. In A Grain of Wheat Wambuku signifies the idea of African independence. She is first the girlfriend and then becomes the wife of Kihiga. She loves him more as a lover than as a husband.

In *The White Veil*, Ogot stands as immoral woman disregarding man's natural impulses. Achola's reluctance stands for easy-going attitude of a Victorian. The relation between Ogot and Achola implies Victorian notion that for real sexual pleasure one needs to look beyond the matrimonial bed.

Miria in *No Bride Price* is a symbol of causality. With the exception of Miria, all the girlfriends are well educated. Although she is an illiterate, she comprehends Lombe's personal problems. Her sympathy and comprehension excel his social status and perception. Agnes Akilo in *Man of the People* is professional and intellectual though culturally inferior. Chief Nanga attracted many women by his wealth and status as Minister but Agnes could attract him.

Girlfriends stand in contrast with the most complex goodtime girls. Remy in contrast with Gloria is psychic and not very serious without any emotional stress. Mercy has dual personality, one as a taxi driver and the other as an influential politician. Unlike the goodtime girls, she is not promiscuous. Selina in *Ripples in the Pool* is regarded as a goodtime girl for two reasons. Firstly, her sexual relationship materially rewarded her. Secondly, she gives bodily pleasure to her patients while nursing them. Hers is a split and disturbed personality. She dies not as a wife nor as a goodtime girl but as a courtesan.

Adaku in Buchi Emecheta's *The Joys of Motherhood* symbolizes the struggle of woman to free herself from the destructive traditional social dogmas that make her a wife primarily to suffer. She seeks to continue casual relationship with men for material gains and physical gratification.

Some African women are portrayed as literate and legally married wives, some assertive and some submissive. Fatima, wife of Dr. Amilo Kanu in Ike's *Sunset at Dawn*, is a university graduate with enough knowledge of medicines to deal effectively with the villagers' problems caused by malnutrition. She is educated like her husband, and enjoys herself in the company of westernized and sophisticated people. Yaniya in Ekwensi's *Beautiful Feathers* is portrayed as smart, good-looking, glamour girl. Edzi in Selor Mey's *The Narrow Path* besides being self-centred is a happy married woman taking care of her children, and unconcerned about her husband's lapses. In Achebe's *A Man of the People*, Chief Nanga's wife is generous and assertive in her own way.

Chinua Achebe in his story, "Marriage is a Private Affair," which he wrote in his youth, dramatizes the problems faced by a young couple who get married ignoring their traditional custom and belief. He talks of the practice of finding a suitable girl by the parents in traditional society. Nnaemeka's father from his native village writes a letter to his son that he had gone and found a girl for him:

> I have found a girl who will suit you admirably. . . .She has a proper Christian upbringing. When she stopped schooling some years ago, her father (a man of sound judgment) sent her to live in the house of a pastor where she has received all the training a wife could need. Her Sunday school teacher has told me that she reads her Bible very fluently.[4]

But Nnaemeka says that he cannot marry his father's choice, as he has already loved Nene Atang, who is a teacher in a Girl's School in Lagos. His father wonders,

> Teacher, did you say? If you consider that a qualification for a good wife I should like to point out to you, Nnaemeka that no Christian woman should teach. St. Paul in his letter to the Corinthians says that woman should keep silence. (*Ibid*)

Flora Nwapa's Idu in *Idu* is lovable and submissive, a believer of male inheritance. She even forces her husband to go for a second marriage when she fails to conceive. But her husband Adiewer does not evince interest in the second marriage. When he falls sick, Idu nurses him with least protest and dies twenty-eight days after his death.

In Emecheta's *The Second Class Citizen* Adah is an intellectual, a superior being. But to Londoners she appears to be just a black immigrant with no proper education. Adah is the property of her husband though she is denied western education. She is the victim of gender discrimination. She supports not only her children but also helps Francis in prosecuting his studies further. She faces many challenges in life and tries to protect and preserve her womanhood. In the novel *The Journey Within*, Ejiaka is a symbol of compassion, joy and Christian faith and she realizes that man is a must in the life of woman.

In Achebe's *Things Fall Apart* Okonkwo's three wives stand for endurance, beauty and anger. His first wife, Nwoye's mother has all the patience to compromise with life and is most obliging to her husband. When Ikemefuna is to be sacrificed, though she inwardly wants to save him she can not spell it out to her husband. She patiently suffers the loss of Ikemefuna. Okonkwo's second wife Ekwefi, whom he won by participating in a wrestling match, stands for beauty. Ojiugo, the third wife of Okonkwo, quite often loses her temper.

In Okpewho's, The Victims Nwabunor is a dominant character craving for power and assaulting her drunkard husband. In Ngugi Thiong'o's The Mubenzi Tribesman, Ruth is socially superior with enough self-confidence and much sophistication. Nwapa's Amaka in *One is Enough* is a rebel fighting back and beating her husband black and blue until he faints. Unlike other women who wish to be submissive, she turns violent and hits him in the chest when she comes to know about his 'secret family'. She becomes conscious of her victimization and as an empirical right she strives to liberate herself from the clutches of cultural bondage.

> When Amaka learns about her husband's secret family, she expresses shock, outrage and disappointment. Her anger is not directed at the second wife because Amaka herself considered another wife for Obiora in order to obtain the requisite children. Obiora does not apologize for his deceit, and their conservation turns into a shouting match. Amaka, a woman has only two choices of behaviour in this situation. She either becomes hysterical or passively accepts his blows. Amaka beats Obiora in the chest. Obiora literally falls on his back.[5]

A free woman is one who flouts the conventional norms and for whom woman is not just to marry and produce children. The most sought after heroine who symbolizes women's protest is Flora Nwapa's *Efuru.* Efuru determines to lead a lonely life without husband when she fails to conceive. Efuru as a rebel, decision-maker and a social reformer desires to change social conventions that affect her own future. She negotiates with all possibilities and remains firm in her decision though other women are angry with her and criticize her for her indifference. She declares emphatically, "I want to be nurtured and sustained by the strengths of my culture but I am also prepared to make changes if any when the need arises."[6] Efuru wants to be a free woman in the real sense of the term. She defines life as she wills and decides: "Life for her meant living it fully. She did not want merely to exist. She wanted to live and use the world to her advantage." (94)

Akunna in Buchi Emecheta's *The Bride Price* flouts the norms of society that a girl must accept as husband the groom chosen for her by her people and that the bride price must be paid before marriage. She marries Chike, her own choice against the will of her father. She wants to lead an independent life and keep her individuality. On the other hand, Dipoko's heroine Ewudu in *Because of Women* not only flouts the traditional norms but also social custom of marriage because of the restrictions imposed on women. The readers view Ewudu as a woman of 'new' ideas in a positive sense. In From *A Crooked Rib*, Farah's heroine Ebla becomes a prostitute not intentionally but in forced circumstances. Yet she is considered to be a free woman.

Cyprian Ekwensi's heroine Beatrice *In People of the City* is a contrast to Ebla. She is a product of circumstánces. She is rich and fond of high life. She plays the roles of goodtime girl and courtesan. Beatrice is compelled to become a free woman due to lack of economic resources. Ekwensi's Enu in *Iska* is also a free woman, though idealistic, and refuses to comply with the traditional standards. June in Kahiga's *The Girl from Abroad* emerges as the passionate deeply-stirred young woman reluctant to marry. She is the incarnation of independence.

For Nnu Ego in Buchi Emecheta's *The Joys of Motherhood*, village stands for infertility and city a place for conceiving but ironically she becomes a victim of politics. On her way back to her room, Nnu Ego felt that she was a prisoner, imprisoned by her love for children, and caged as the senior wife. She cannot ask for money for the maintenance of household as it was considered below the standard of a woman in her position. She felt the attitude of men unfair as men cleverly used woman's sense of responsibility only to enslave her.

Mother is but the incarnation of love. African women, though detached from their husbands, try to retain motherly instinct. Women also advise their husbands to get a second wife to become mothers to their children. Nnu Ego in Emecheta's *Joys of Motherhood* is a pain-stricken mother who struggles hard to rear her children, and she even sacrifices her life for their welfare. She defines the validity of her womanhood solely by the success of her children. Buchi Emecheta, not satisfied with the image of mother, offers a positive image of women by encouraging their education. According to her, "Women are capable of living for so many other reasons than men."[7] Nnu Ego sacrifices her life for the sake of children and becomes oblivious of the outer world. She creates a world for herself with the children: "She never really made friends, so busy had she been building up her joys as a mother." (224)

Adaku in *The Joys of Motherhood* too does not believe in the sanctity of marriage. When Nnu Ego asks her about her indifference towards her own daughters, she replies that they are meant to sell themselves in order to look after their family. Her own experience of life induces Adaku to finance for promising education for her daughters, which would make them live on their own without dependence on man for finance.

Flora Nwapa's Idu projects the image of a woman who rejects cultural tradition, male dominance and primacy of the child even though portrayed as passive, powerless, passionless, unimaginative and irresponsible woman. Idu is portrayed both as a loyal wife and devout mother. Later Idu becomes insane when her son dies, for she could not stand the bereavement.

In Nwapa's novel *Efuru* the two characters, Ossai the mother of Adizua and the protagonist, Efuru stand for maternal love. Ossai as mother, shares the grief of Adizua who could not afford to pay the bride price. Similarly when Adizua starts neglecting Efuru and maintains illicit relationship with another woman, she as dutiful mother tries to check his behaviour. More than Adizua, she grieves over the loss of Efuru when Efuru divorces him. Efuru even disowning her father marries Adizua. But when Adizua fails to attend the funeral of her child, her motherhood compels her to go for divorce. Efuru watched the men as they lowered her only child into the coffin. She stood there like a statue with tears running down her cheeks.

Courtesans are professional love-makers. For them lovemaking is a trade, a trade in flesh. They demand respect and exhibit ability to captivate, seduce people and provide sexual enjoyment, whereas ordinary prostitutes are poverty-stricken, for whom prostitution is their livelihood. But both are paid women, leading immoral life.

Cyprian Ekwensi highlights the worse and more disturbing elements of postcolonial African society with a focus on the stereotyped female images. To create interest in the Western reader, he has made subtle racism and sexism themes of many of his works. In *Jagua Nana*, Jagua is a courtesan of high order. She is professional in her dealings with men. She cherishes her bitter experiences to mean something. Besides being a courtesan, she is also a successful woman. She has assumed four roles of woman—as wife, mother, prostitute and extra breadwinner for the household.

Ekwensi has made Jagua very fascinating, a character with her own life style and thoughts. She is a liberated woman enjoying sexuality. She looks like a jaguar, holds her victims in her so-called "clutches of Jagua." She exhibits her glamour to earn money. Jagua Nana is a seductive prostitute imaged in the corrupt and money-hungry society. She resembles Emile in Zolo's Novel *Nana* and Defoe's *Moll Flanders* in her carefree and wretched life. Like Tom Tulliver in George Elliot's *Mill on the Floss*, Freddie, Jagua Nana's patriarchal brother, upbraids her for the kind of life she leads:

> My dear sister it is time you stop your loose life. Is a shameful thin' to me, your brother, I got a beautiful sister like you. God made you with dignity an' when I think of your kind of life. . . . My sister come home and stay in the family. You don' wan' to marry. Awright. Nobody forcin' you. Den keep yourself with respect.[8]

Ghanaian writer, Ama Ata Aidoo has also dealt with the theme of prostitution in her work *Something to Talk about on the Way to the Funeral*. She narrates the story of Auntie Araba, an independent thinker, who goes in search of a job in order to feed her family. She conceives by the barrister she works for. In anger and out of contempt, unable to bear the bitter truth, she turns into a prostitute.

Moral corruption as a theme dominates the literary scene in African fiction. In postcolonial Nigeria, Ghana and Kenya, the westernized woman is looked upon as 'cheap' and 'available' and her presence in the job market is seen as a threat that can only be contended with accusations of sexual permissiveness. In African society, prostitution is not a matter of concern though its primary occupation is agriculture and it encouraged early marriage and early child bearing. It is the rich that indulge in concubinage and polygamy. In many places, women are subjected to sexual harassment, prostitution and consequent endemic venereal diseases. Women are treated as common wealth to be shared by many. Even for the police, prostitution has become a source of income. The White also do not spare black women. They have illicit relationship with black women.

Wole Soyinka also presents the stereotyped images of women that fall into one of the three categories: the foolish virgin in rural settings, the *femme fatale* in urban settings and the masculanised matron. According to Davies, Soyinka's works present the kernel of positive portrayal of female image that is never fully realized.

In Soyinka's *The Interpreters*, Simi unlike Jagua is an intelligent and pleasure-seeking woman. As a courtesan, she is satisfied. Ekwensi's character Konni in Loko Town is a progressive woman, experienced practitioner, and an independent thinker. In Ekwensi's words: "She lived alone, she paid her rent, and did just as she pleased." Her main purpose of prostitution is to regain respectability.

In Mwangi's *Going down Riverside*, Wini is an illegitimate woman, solely engaged in prostitution in order to sustain her child. She never goes to bed with every casual contact she makes. She behaves for sometime truly as their legitimate wife, professionally she is a semi-skilled worker. In Ngugi's *Minutes of Glory*, Beatrice, a downtrodden, is the protagónist. When subjected to humiliation time and again, she realizes that good looks alone can attract people and make woman successful. An ordinary virtuous woman becomes a professional prostitute.

Women that flouted traditional norms turned into politicians. Penda, a prominent character in Ousmane's *God's Bits of Wood*, markedly signifies a woman who is politically active and independent. Right from her childhood, she disguised herself more as a boy. When a man slapped her, she retaliated slapping on his face. And she actively participated in strikes.

People believe that Penda has 'heart and stomach' of a man, masculine in temperament. This African novel with rural setting depicts traditional culture and woman in her traditional role. The characters in the modern urban setting look different by their extreme individualism. They are considered as single, isolated, unified, culturally free-thinking individuals reflecting urban individualism in the society in transition. The characters are self-confident and rely on the inner voice. They are exposed to several crises in their society and try to solve their problems independently. Ama Ata Aidoo's Esi in *Changes* is an independent working woman symbolizing female protest. Esi is also a dutiful and obliging daughter and granddaughter. African woman, besides playing the roles of mother, wife, whore, courtesan, prostitute, daughter and neighbour, has also become a political leader and a professional worker.

Soyinka and Achebe's characters exhibiting integrity and moral austerity boldly face the brutalities of degenerating male-dominated society. The degree of resistance in extremity sometimes involves serious physical loss and even death. Their self-assertion vindicates their individuality. Achebe has presented the image of an idealized woman, thereby opening the space for women to become active and involve themselves along with men in the nation-building activities. They are the images of progressive women though they are not fully evolved characters.

In most of the literary texts, women slander, backstab and hurt one another. But in Achebe's works, women do not indulge in violence against other women. Further, these multiple images of women shift constantly unlike the stereotyped women in traditional society. And it becomes difficult for the black woman to define her identity and her specific role in the given changed circumstances.

NOTES

1. Camara Laye, *The Dark Child* (New York: Farrar, Straus and Giroux, 1954).
2. Chinua Achebe, *Things Fall Apart* (London: Heinemann, 1958), 95.
3. Flora Nwapa, *Mammy Water* (Tana, 1979).
4. Chinua Achebe, *Girls at War and Other Stories* (1972).
5. Flora Nwapa, *One is Enough* (London: Heinemann, 1981), 41.
6. Flora Nwapa, *Efuru* (London: Heinemann, 1966).
7. Buchi Emecheta, *The Joys of Motherhood* (New York: Brazallier, 1979).
8. Cyprian Ekwensi, *Jagua Nana* (London: Heinemann, 1961), 105.

Chapter IV

Feminism in West African Novel

The term feminism signifies action against oppression, discrimination, and violence encountered by women and is broadly described as a belief in the social, political and economic equality of the sexes. According to Oxford Advanced Learner's Dictionary, 'feminism' is the belief and aim that woman should have the same rights and opportunities as men; the struggle to achieve this aim. Chambers' 20th Century Dictionary defines the term 'feminism' as an idiom or expression characteristic of woman: addiction to feminine ways.

Feminism today is not just the forte of the West, but it has found its way into literatures of other countries also. Male-centred aesthetics and their hegemony of the masculine perspective are now being challenged in the writings of African-American women. Black women, being at once black, poor and female have been victimized by racism, sexism and capitalism, not only from the White world but also from the men of their own black world. As Barbara Smith observes, the black women are bearers of "geometric oppression" and bear race, gender and class—a triple consciousness. Paul Marshall stands out as a pioneer of the black women's renaissance in the field of Afro-American literature. In South African context, women in the works of Nadine Gordimer are under serious political and domestic constraints and their struggle is not totally against their men who are themselves oppressed as helpless, but much against the system.

Feminism seeks to remove gender inequalities and create an egalitarian society where women are given equal and uniform treatment by the society. But the term was misunderstood giving rise to misconceptions and false propaganda that it is meant to hate the authority of men. The chief objective of feminism as a movement is to accomplish specific goals to bring awareness in women about their just rights and to oppose male domination in all spheres of life. Contemporary feminism is an ideology that tries to define woman's place in the social pattern. In the patriarchal society, woman is defined and differentiated with reference to man and not with reference to her; she is the incidental, the inessential as opposed to the essential. He is the subject; he is the Absolute—she is the other. Indeed, such a placement and scaling down of woman is the crux of Western feminism.

Feminism as a movement is to check domestic violence and to work for economic development by identifying feminist issues and problems. It also means to encourage women to assert themselves, thereby challenging some of the practices that affected their individuality and subordinates their position in their own society. It means that women too are capable and have the right to make their own decisions and choose their own course of advancement.

Feminism is a notion that cuts the barriers deliberately formed to prevent the progress and affect the interests of women. It worked for the self-realization of women and for parity with men and similar participation in all developmental activities. It is an effort made by a group of committed women writers in a single voice to counter women degradation due to sex discrimination and supposed lack of individuality. Women writers try to educate women about their condition of life and goals. It is a voice raised against the degrading attitude of men towards women and sounds more than philosophy; it is a fight against female sexual oppression and exploitation.

Feminism is generally viewed as a constructive effort made to resist women oppression and a commitment to struggle for women's liberation from all kind of atrocities—internal, external, psychological, emotional, socio-economic, political, philosophical and discrimination based on race, class and culture. It aims at conferring dignity, social status on women and it opposes the traditional customs that degrade women and that are detrimental to their progress. In order to curb too much male assertion, it has disguised itself as female chauvinism. It sensitized women to advance in life. According to Gloria Steinem,

> Feminism is no simple reform. It really is a revolution. Sex and race because they are easy and visible differences have been the primary ways of organizing human beings into superior and inferior groups and into the cheap labour in which the system still survives. We are talking about a society in which there will be no roles other than those chosen or those earned. We are really talking about the humanism.[1]

Pearl S Buck opines that the society exists based on the healthy familial relations, in particular between men and women. "The basic discovery about any people is the discovery of the relationship between its men and its women."[2] Elaine Heffner feels that the expansion of women into selfhood, motherhood and self-esteemed individual is possible only through liberation of women.

Women do not have to sacrifice personhood if they are mothers. They do not have to sacrifice motherhood in order to be persons. Liberation is meant to expand women's opportunities not to limit them. The self-esteem that has been found in new pursuits can also be found in mothering.[3] Susan B. Anthony slyly remarks that there should be parity between the two genders. "Men, their rights, and nothing more; women, their rights, and nothing less."[4]

Even today, in the United States of America, women are being discriminated against on the basis of gender, colour and economic status. Women with similar qualifications are paid less than their male counterparts for the same job and further women are restricted in choosing their employment. Woman is harassed and victimized. There are woman enslavement practised in the closed tradition-bound societies in Afghanistan and women are forced to wear burka from head to toe. Also in India, in orthodox societies, in different parts of the country, women find similar ill treatment, insubordination and enslavement to so-called tradition and 'shariyath' in Muslim community. Widows are but non-entities in their own families. Though education and cultural reforms have changed the mindset and outlook of the people in some places, the old attitudinal patterns continue in other places. Widows are still considered a bad omen in certain modern societies. In orthodox families, they are not allowed to perform certain rituals and participate in celebrations.

The status of women in rural areas is different from that in urban society. In villages, women are either confined to kitchen or allowed to assist their spouse in farming. They are not consulted in decision-making, nor are they allowed to remarry. The Indian society is also basically a male-dominated society. Indian feminism is obviously critical about marriage, orthodoxy and anti-male domination. Even in the United States of America, some of the well-qualified, English-speaking Indian women, when they join their husbands on H-I B visa, face many restrictions. They are often forced to remain indoors and are subjected to domestic violence and abuse, physical and psychological repression. They are denied to take up employment of their choice under the provisions of the H-4 spouse visa and thus are deprived of economic independence and are not allowed to get back to their native country to lead an independent life.

Women, nearly half of the 37.2 million adult populations, suffer from HIV, a serious threat to mankind as a whole, because of lack of education, economic dependence and sexual harassment. Kathleen Cravero, Deputy Executive Director of the Joint United Nations Programme on HIV/AIDS (UNAIDS) says,

> Increasingly the face of AIDS is young and female. Young women are almost an endangered species in Southern Africa from AIDS for several reasons. Many women have no access to education or jobs. They are often economically dependent on men and may not have the power to resist sex, or ask their husbands or partner to use a condom.[5]

The main HIV risk factor on the increase in women is because they are loyal and submissive to their husbands though they have illicit relations with other women. Even girls in their teenage are acquiring the virus from affected male because of sexual violence. In South Asian context, feminism is described as an awareness of women suppression and exploitation at the place of work and within the family, and it emerged as a conscious effort made by women and men to change the situation and attitude of the society towards women. A feminist discriminating a traditional woman from a modern woman said:

> A traditional woman in Africa is one who is dumb enough to live with polygamist in a remote village and speak Igbo, Wolof, Twi, Yoruba, or some other African language, while a modern woman is one who is able to leave her husband and move to city and speak / write English, Spanish or French.[6]

The role of African woman in agriculture, trade and other economic pursuits is constructive and supportive to her family and society. Though she works for more than eighteen hours like men, yet she is deprived of her right to property and she cannot make financial transactions independently. Harrison has rightly observed that woman is so heavily burdened throughout the third world that it becomes a Herculean task to redress her grievances in much of Africa.

African women strain more but are paid less money. They are vulnerable to serious diseases. The trappings of sophistication and to maintain social status lure sometimes even elite women and for show off, they subject themselves to moral deprivation. Women, though equally qualified, are denied jobs in the fields of engineering, computer technology, architecture and medicine for no valid reason. Adding to their woes, child marriages are common in certain communities. Female literacy in Africa is poor as in Arab states and South Asia. In Nigeria, mostly educated women prefer to become teachers though they have but limited opportunities to progress. Slowly the situation in Africa too is changing. Women are going for higher education, joining technical courses and also seeking self-employment.

The emergence of feminism can be traced to the early twentieth century when some so-called feminist women committed themselves to certain issues of women, such as equal rights, personal freedom, economic independence, parity with men and emancipation from social and familial bondage. Feminists are deeply concerned with and about uplift of women in society.

They advocate personal freedom for self-fulfillment and have even demanded the entry of women into all those domains where men constitute the only work force.

Economic independence is most essential to assert oneself and for personal advancement, as held by Charlotte Perkins Gilman, the foremost feminist intellectual of the early twentieth century. In her famous book *Women and Economics* (1898), she argues that only when women achieved economic independence, further racial progress would be assured. She supports the idea of married career women and the modernization of second marriage by assigning housekeeping and relegating tasks such as cooking, laundry and child-care at home to professionals.

The younger feminists hold the view that the life of women just for some biological differentiation is culturally conditioned for insubordination. Sexual emancipation, according to Emma Goldman, is required more than the winning of legal rights for women. Gilman views sex as drain on intellectual achievement and a threat to personal autonomy. Goldman declares that the greatest shortcoming of the emancipation of woman today lies in its artificial stiffness and its narrow respectability, which produce an emptiness in woman's soul that will not let her drink from the fountain of life and that the demand for equal rights in every vocation of life is just and fair. But after all, the most vital right is the right to love and be loved.

It is worth-noting that African-American women too have insisted on gender equality and many early feminist women who once championed the cause of women gave up their struggle after sometime. But a new phrase developed disowning their status. *"I am not a feminist, but. . . ."* is a phrase that encouraged and organized possible activity to bring about change in society.

Talking about feminism in Africa Professor Amina Mama, one of Africa's leading contemporary feminist scholars, the Chairperson of Gender Studies and Director of the African Gender Institute (AGI), tells about her personal journey into feminism. She says that she has often been called a feminist, and she has confessed that Rebecca Mae West has influenced her. Whenever she does something contrary to tradition and domestic convention, people call her a feminist. Sometimes the term remained unpalatable for its anti-democratic interests. The so-called 'imperial feminism' evoked much response from different sections of society and was debated for consensus. African regimes have encouraged gender politics and misrepresented feminism. And African societies too have failed to perceive the concept of 'feminism' and its importance in community development. Amina Mama, ignoring the antagonistic attitude of the society, as a feminist committed to the cause of women, took up the responsibility of bettering the condition of life of African women.

Identifying herself with feminism, Amina Mama says that feminism has emerged as a positive and constructive movement and it is a social commitment to struggle for liberation of women from all kinds of oppression. Amina Mama likes the word 'feminist' because it identifies her with a community of confident and radical women, many of whom she respects, both as individuals and for their contribution to the development.

Talking about the relevance of womanism to African feminists, she says that the term was coined by Alice Walker, an American woman of colour, as a critique of and her response to white-dominated feminism. In the USA, white domination is most visible to women of colour like Walker. It is quite evident that the most salient thing to black women living in the West is racism, and they feel like alienating themselves from the white. Even in white-dominated contexts, she feels that the white feminism conflicts with the northern-based white women's monopoly of feminism.

Amina Mama wants a delinking of Women's Movements from Feminism in African context. Women's liberation requires thorough addressing of gender injustice from micro- to the macro-political level, and not shying away from any level of struggle. She suggests the ways to address the issues pertaining to the disturbing trend in anti-intellectualism among some women activists. She further tells that much emphasis is on engaging women with theory and analysis from an activist perspective instead of leaving them to continue to face perpetrating intellectual and epistemic violence against them.

Twentieth Century Women Liberation Movement:

Americans earlier thought that women were generally weak and were just a means of procreation. "Some nations believe that women ought to be protected because they are weak, but we know the truth, women must be protected because they have the strength to carry the pains of creation."[7] But people who speak of liberation should realize that it is possible only through women's emancipation. President Sekov Toure feels that in the emancipation of women is the emancipation of men.

African women's movement gains momentum only when it educates, mobilizes, organizes African women folk successfully. Liberation movements like Anglo LAN women movement, a popular movement for the liberation of Angola, united people together and led to the unification of women for their own emancipation from cultural male-domination. A conference was held to approve and declare women's liberation movement as International Women's Day. But the women's struggle for liberation remained dormant in nineteen twenties.

In the nineteen sixties, Women's Liberation Movement became popular and appealed to the public conscience. It created a sensation in the United States of America as a social movement. Women's Liberation Movement developed into two distinct streams. The first was the National Organization for Women 1966 (NOW). They were highly traditional with their own strategy to claim equality with men for jobs and to become part of the work force. National conferences were held by this organization and it fought against gender discrimination.

The second was called Women's movement comprising mostly young women graduates from colleges who had been active in the anti-war and civil rights movements. This movement was meant to change the social life of women and encounter male-dominated power structure in the society. This was more publicized through sit-ins, street theatres, poetry and songs, speak-outs, irreverent images and slogans.

Historically, the black African women are the most suppressed lot in the United States for they are discriminated in their own patriarchal community by the black male and racially discriminated and sexually exploited by the white male and further they are also forced to become subservient to the white woman. This led to African woman's psychological depression, which she has meekly accepted as her fate, destined not to become a free individual. Her plight is ascribed to her economic dependence and her adherence to traditional responsibility of sustaining her family. In nineteen sixty-five, the United States government published a booklet entitled *The Negro Family—The Case for National Action* (1965). The author of the booklet states that in essence, the Negro community has been forced into matriarchal structure, because it is so out of time with the rest of American society, which retards the progress of the group as a whole.

Contrary to the popular opinion, black woman under slavery on the American soil underwent a process of de-socialization adopting a new culture and a language. All Black women resisted the sexual advances made by white men and allowed their exploitation only to save and support their family. Many black women realized that together with their men, they would have to fight against colour discrimination and economic exploitation by the Whites.

Feminists insisted that violence against women should not become a public political issue like rape, incest, domestic violence and sexual harassment. By early nineteen seventies, black feminism progressed and gave impetus to women's liberation movement, thus creating a free space for exploring personal and sexual issues which lesbians felt free to express themselves. Leaders of the movement were scared that lesbians would degrade and dilute the spirit of feminism.

Women Liberation Movement expected good response from black women too. The frustrated women started alienating themselves from their men and black women started showing little concern for the things 'American'. This caused a change in the attitude of men towards women both in America and Africa. Feminist movements educated women to fight for better treatment and equal wages for similar work and men were compelled to share the responsibility of the household and child-rearing when the women went out to work. Gradually by 1980s and

1990s, women were treated as equals. Women felt that without another world war, the world recognized the intensity of their suffering and put an end to their centuries-long degradation and male domination.

African Feminism

African feminism is an emerging model, conception of concerns of black women born of female discourse. It deals with sexism, totalitarianism and ethnic prejudice. Prominent nineteenth century feminists such as Sojourner Truth, Mary Ann Shaddcary, Harriet Tubman and Lucy C. Laney marked the beginning of Black feminism in the United States of America. They encouraged the black women to emotionally advance and become politically conscious. And subsequently African-American women of twentieth century turned black feminism into a political movement, intellectual voice and vision of fulfillment.

African women became in course of time self-reliant, independent and resourceful and Black feminism emerged as a self-conscious struggle leading to the realization of humanistic vision of a community; as a voice against suppression and oppression; and a revolution which was anti-sexist, anti-racist and anti-elitist. In other words, it is for human empowerment, empowerment of black women. Black feminism has revealed black women's historical attention in four core themes—the legacy of struggle, the search for voice, the interdependence of thought and action and significance of empowerment in everyday life.

Legacy of struggle against the suppression in the society led to the awareness among black intellectuals to think about the race, class, gender differences and women's suffering. It differentiates white women from black women. Search for voice or the refusal of women to remain silenced reveals black women's inferiority and ineffectuality. It comprises four controlling images of a black woman—the mammy, the matriarch, the welfare mother, and jezebel, which reflect the dominant group's interests in maintaining black woman's subordination. Their own community and outsiders view black women negatively as well. However, the portrayal of positive images acts as a source of inspiration and fount of strength to black women.

The interdependence of thought and action is black women's political activism. They have merged the two forms of expression—orientation of views and thought and action as a part of the same process. The thought and action makes black women visualize oppression and bitter experiences, to develop self-defined voice against suppressions and to become self-reliant. The empowerment in everyday life is quite necessary to encounter the challenges pertaining to race, gender and class oppression and the collective action is the only solution to eradicate long-standing political, social and economic inequalities.

Black feminism in the twentieth century got diversified into a national political movement, a movement for transformation and contemporary awareness. National political movement raised intellectual voice for civil rights, end of terrorism and adequate standard of living. The growth of black urban community led to the foundation of black women's club movement and change occurred in the working class in which black women advanced the humanistic vision in black feminist thought primarily within African-American communities. The contemporary period analyzed subjects such as the struggle for education, sexual politics, violence, race, pride, racial, prejudice etc. African women, portrayed as overburdened with domestic work and also with caring animals and families, are the negative images that they hated.

Cooper, a black woman, a recipient of an M.A. degree from Oberlin College and a Ph.D. from Sorbonne in Paris, works as educator. Her book *A Voice From the South* (1892) has described the black women's legacy of struggle against racism and sexism by protesting black women's vulnerability to sexual violence. She says that she would beg to add her plea for the coloured girls of the South: the large, bright, promising fatally beautiful class, so full of promise and possibilities, yet so sure of destruction; often without a father to whom they dare apply the loving term, often without a stronger brother to espouse their cause and defend their honour with his life's blood; in the midst of pitfalls and snares, waylaid by the lower classes of white men with no shelter or protection. Williams viewed the black women not as a defenceless victim but as a strong-willed resistor as meanly as she is thought of, hindered as she is in all directions, she is always doing something of merit and credit that is not expected of her.

The period from 1920 to 1960 has not been very significant in protecting the interests of women. Everyday activity of black women reflected some aspect of feminism. Black feminism in the later period articulated black women's agenda and led to the formation of an organizational base to effectively present the themes of black feminism. Black feminism raised its voice against the long-standing illness restricting women's freedom and their participation in socio-cultural activities and in the last quarter of the twentieth century the trends of black feminism fostered an attitudinal change. Firstly, the increasing social class distinction led to the thinking of black women and secondly, social class satisfaction resulted in black feminist concern. Tony Cade Bambara's *The Black Woman: An Anthology* in 1970 pioneered the black feminist agenda. Toni Morison's novel *The Bluest Eye* (1970) and Alice Walker's novel *Meridian* (1976) also echoed the black women issues.

Catherine McKinnon states that sexuality is the focus point of male power. Radical feminists have grudgingly pointed out that women's suppression is because of the disparity in gender relationship found in sexual asymmetry and the sexual division of labour and in the patriarchal and universal male control and women's sexual procreative capacity. According to Katherine Frank, novels by African women writers are concerned with the contemporary African woman who can negotiate her way between the claims of tradition and modernization.

Most feminists have advocated empowerment of women initially in their family. Motherhood is a theme that dominates the writings of many African women writers who pose a question: Are women merely forced mothers or sexual objects. They point out that women's sexuality is controlled by an unbalanced sexual division of labour that manipulates woman's procreative activities on one hand and on the other woman's body presented as a pleasure-based entity that has either been suppressed or repressed.

Feminist criticism works as a device to analyze feminism further in the context of literature and cultural angularities of different nations. It focuses on women, their biographical, historical studies, women writers and women audience and women's issues portrayed in individual literature. Hazel Carby's article, "White Women Listen? Black Feminism and the Boundaries of Sisterhood," deals with the black women's historiography reconstituting the power and privilege of black women. Feminist critics probe into the feminist verbiage. A feminist critic must necessarily be an outsider with an unbiased scholarship fostering intellectual maturity and possible social changes. Feminist concerns uphold patriarchal system oppressing women and subjecting them to sexual exploitation. Feminist critical theory as a formal, legitimate and analytical tool, helps in the contextual and structural analysis.

Feminist critics of African literature have chosen African women as slaves to the African traditions for study and probing. African women seem to shout in one voice, "Knock down the traditions and save the men." Feminist critics focus primarily on the rebellious nature of women to liberate themselves from tradition-bound African society. True feminists, who believe in possibilities, make possibilities happen. Feminist critics look at Nwapa's Efuru as a reformer than a rebel, an agent of change, even to alter the rules for her own good. Even though the radical feminist goes against African traditions, an Igbo adheres to his culture to keep its organic nature for its strengths and advantages.

Elaine Showalter in his book *A Literature of Their Own* classifies feminist theory into Androgynist poetics, Feminist critique, Female aesthetic and Gynocrities. Androgynist poetics emerged in the mid-Victorian women's writings and the main purpose was to uphold the female virtues, women given to imagination without prejudice. Feminist critique analyzed the male-oriented society subjecting women to oppression and treating women as inferior. Another form of feminist theory manifested itself into the female aesthetics relating to the female consciousness colliding against her own self; 'something about the body, about the passions.'

Gynocriticism does not approve of female identity and style. It tries to trace the ideological inscriptions and the literary effects of gender system. Feminism is prominent as a critique to counter in literature the misrepresentations of women struggling for education, for improved economic status for survival, their motherhood in domestic sphere and as responsible members of community to participate in politics and support their men in revolution and of their demand for better treatment by men.

African women have greater roles to perform as a writer, as a woman and as a third world person. Feminine writing has developed its own style since it has a specific purpose, a social transformation, and a change in the attitude of male towards their counterparts. And thus feminist scholarship fosters intellectual maturity for social change. The feministic representation sometimes appears to be harsh and rude but only to caution men who are arrogant and indifferent and inhuman to women and hinder their intellectual growth and social and economic advancement.

African Feminist critics are dogmatic on certain aspects of African feminism, like radical feminism that opposed portrayal of woman in literature as non-entity and ineffective being and are keen on exhibiting potential of African woman. Honor Tracy, a British woman, made implacable observations in her critical review of *Things Fall Apart* in 1958. Achebe himself was impatient with such sarcasm by the Blacks about blacks questioning their integrity and cultural affiliation. He wonders how these bright Negro barristers who talk gullibly about African culture would like to return to wearing raffia skirts.

African literary texts are quite complex. Our selective and one-dimensional readings are superficial. Instead of going into the complexities of the text, some feminists choose to engage themselves in questioning the selectivity akin to prosecution and declaring the defendant guilty even before the trial begins. The pervasive selectivity of the criticism renders validity, authenticity and legitimacy. Critics of Achebe's *Things Fall Apart* are silent about Okonkwo's actions even though he transgressed the norms of the Igbo traditional society and beat his wife in the Peace Week and was harsh to his women and children. Okonkwo is rude and gives himself to rage on several occasions. During the Peace Week, when his wife Ojiugo goes to her friend's house to plait her hair and returns late, Okonkwo becomes furious and starts bullying and beating her. He considers her only as an object of subjugation but her intolerance and reaction come as a rude shock.

Feminists try to shield female characters from thorough scrutiny and reprimand. The illusion of sisterhood that tossed over the complexities of women's lives in the first decade of the second wave of feminism causing much pain becomes a moral lesson to the feminists. Throughout the literary texts, women slander, backstab and cause pain to one another but Achebe's works are an exception since his women are only at the receiving end as victims of violence.

Florence Stratton writes that the central divinity in Achebe's Umuofia is represented by Ani, the goddess of earth, but Ani doesn't protect the interests of women. Though Okonkwo commits an outrage against Ani by beating his youngest wife during the Peace Week, Ani does not punish him for his male brutality. Feminist critics strike a similarity between the Igbo goddess and the policemen. Feminist criticism of African literature always aims at heralding the emergence of the rebellious African woman.

Rosie O'Donnell and Hillary Clinton say that women never defend men always since they keep themselves busy in counting the spoils gained on their behalf by the feminists. Family law says that women are always guaranteed three quarters of the property and are the sole custodian of their children most of the time simply by pleading womanhood. For the past forty years men have had a set back and allowed themselves to be browbeaten into submission and castrated by feminists. Female critics opine that the need to liberate African people from neocolonialism and other forms of race and class oppression is coupled with respect for certain features of traditional African culture.

The feminist consciousness craves for recognition of women as individuals in the contemporary African societies. Feminist criticism broadens the literary cannon by introducing the literature of African women in the changed social set-up. Western feminist critics also speak of their own heightened awareness and the concerns of the authors and their works. They use sociological, linguistic, psychoanalytic and historical approaches to give a wider perspective of womanism in African literature.

The Feminist criticism tends to probe into several historical and biographical studies of women of different countries and communities. Feminism remains a positive movement since it has committed itself to the struggle for emancipation of woman from all bondages and forms of oppression—internal, external, psychological, emotional, socio-economic, political and philosophical. In the society dominated by the Whites, white women try to assert themselves and champion their cause for the uplift of women in general. Western feminists have a strong feeling that women in different societies are exposed to the onslaughts of the society based on class, race and culture reflected in gender relations.

Most feminists discriminate sex from gender and sex is understood as a person's biological maleness or femaleness, while gender refers to the non-physiological aspects of sex, a group of attributes or behavioural patterns shaped by society and culture. Some feminists have argued that gender is a socio-cultural process involving a complex set of relations that inevitably interlock with other relations of age, race, class, ethnicity, ideology etc.

In Chinua Achebe's *Things Fall Apart*, in the household of Okonkwo, his first wife occupies prime position even after Okonkwo's having two more wives, namely Ekwefi and Ojiugo. Okonkwo as a mark of respect never calls his first wife by her name like the other two. Moreover she is addressed as Nwoye's mother. During the Peace Week, she is the first to offer Kola nut to Ani, the goddess of Earth. Okonkwo eats the food sent by

Nwoye's mother first and then relishes the dishes of the other two wives.

African gender exhibits inequality between women and between the spouses. Gender discriminates one from the other in every respect like education, work, socio-economic status, marriage, decision-making powers, mobility, domestic violence and political participation by African women. Men enjoy all the privileges in the patriarchal society whereas women are mostly the deprived lot.

Educational deprivation is common for gender discrimination, and even for similar work they are paid less. For their total economic dependency on male, they can't go against the will of their men. Extreme chronic poverty is because of large family, economic dependence, lack of viable options outside marriage and a deeply entrenched culture of male authority that makes domestic violence endemic in Africa. They have their say only in showing the accounts of expenditure related to income and investment.

Participation of women in politics means casting their vote during the elections. They find no proper place or position in the administration except attending election meetings and in participating in the election campaign for the candidature mostly of men. Their services to the family and society go unrecognized and unacknowledged. In *Imperial Leather*, Anne McClintock argues that to understand gender one must recognize that

> race, gender and class are not distinct realms of experience, existing in splendid isolation from each other; nor can they be simply yoked together retrospectively like armatures of Lego. Rather they come into existence in and through relation to each other —if in contradictory and conflicted ways.[8]

West African Feminism

Mother is supreme. Even the patriarchal African traditional society is governed by the female principle. African woman occupies a significant place though relegated to a secondary place next to male in tradition-bound society unlike in European and Arab countries. Most African women writers do not qualify themselves to be called feminists. Since their feminism does not adequately describe and define their socio-cultural realities, writers like Flora Nwapa and others prefer to be called womanists, a term suggested by Alice Walker to show their allegiance to the struggle of black women in Africa and Diaspora against racism, sexism, and ageism. Though the West African writers do not conform to the specifications of feminists as set by the western feminists, their works offer realistic pictures of gender issues in a patriarchal society.

Flora Nwapa's first two novels *Efuru* in 1966 and *Idu* in 1970 earned her name and reputation as a writer. Nwapa continued her career as an educator. She made use of Nigerian myths to make her modern stories interesting to the outsider. She portrayed strong and individualized women in Nigerian setting in her novels. Her female characters are assertive and take decisions on vital issues of their families and pertaining to the social customs.

Nwapa prefers to present the socio-economic and cultural problems from the female point of view with a view to elevate the status of women in their native society. Her works identify African women's problems and try to give remedial solutions. Her feminism is reflected in defining and interpreting the lives of African women but in an interview with Dr. Akachi Ezeigbo, Nwapa has admitted that she is not imposing any of her feminist characters like Amaka in *One is Enough* on her readers. She says:

> It depends on the motivation I have when portraying a character. In *One is Enough* I was not cut to create a role model in Amaka. I was simply creating a woman who found herself in a corrupt society and struggles to exist there the way she thought the best.[9]

Nwapa's novel *One is Enough* is a replica of Saadawi's work *In Women at Point Zero* and Helen Buckingham's *Women in Crime.* Saadawi in her novel *In Women at Point Zero* has portrayed a prostitute more worthy than a wife. A wife to her is the most exploited slave who foolishly submits herself to her husband even though he is ungrateful while the prostitute is a self-reputed woman and conscious of her position, who exposes the wicked nature of man and cautions him that he would have to pay heavily if would approach her.

Saadawi declares that a woman's life is always miserable. A prostitute, however, is a little better of all and women are prostitutes of one kind or another. The lowest paid body is that of a wife. A successful prostitute is better than a mislaid saint. Marriage is a system built on the cruellest suffering of woman. Similarly Nwapa confesses that a wife's position is less than a prostitute. So Amaka as her mouthpiece prefers to become a prostitute than to remain a submissive wife. Amaka, after beating her husband nearly to death, escapes into the city disowning her husband and breaks marital bonds out of utter contempt for men. The provoked violence forces Amaka question her own beliefs and societal roles: "Was she useless to society if she were not a mother? . . . Was a woman nothing because she was unmarried or barren? Was there no other fulfillment for her?"[10]

She thinks that she is only a woman of substance. But the irony is that the same Amaka who rejects one man who is her husband, willingly and enthusiastically, allows herself to become public property of all men in the city. "Liberation indeed has come! Long live feminism!" Nwapa as an early feminist inspired many women writers in Africa. In the words of Charles Nnolim, the female writers that emerged after Nwapa, never quite freed themselves from Nwapa's janus-faced, confusion-ridden feminist ideology. The novels of Nwapa examined and reviewed many of the prevalent notions of marriage, social responsibility, self-sacrifice, and service to society and humanity. Nwapa's feminine perspective is visualized through her female characters catalyzing the events and the fate of other characters involved in action.

Nwapa's women stand for industry, ingenuity and resilience. Nwapa deals only with successful women and the fate of nation. She initiated 'womanisation' of Nigerian letters. Nwapa's distinctive concern is the inter-relationship of life and death, which has become a landmark in Nigerian literature. It is thematically recreated in the birth of insanity and the death of pregnant women. She weaves together traditional Igbo and the myths with imported views of women to create complex characters struggling for independence in their societies. She shows how women succeeded outside their traditional roles of mother and wife but reaffirming faith in Igbo culture; Nwapa says that she has been writing for nearly thirty years and her interest has been on both the rural and the urban woman in her quest for survival in a fast-changing world dominated by men.

By breaking the silence of women in Nigerian letters, Nwapa has carved a niche for herself in the twentieth century African women's writing. But Nwapa upholds the androgynous nature of her society. Boldly she exposes the complementary sex role system in Ugwuta society. She has realistically portrayed her women in their traditional roles as shrewd market women, energetic farmers, wealthy traders, decision makers, sharp business entrepreneurs, independent thinkers and powerful respected priestesses.

Her heroines are, of course ideal women but with serious flaws in them that are contrary to the traditional norms and customs. She exhibits firm understanding of the moral issues involved; the betrayal of trust; the insecurity of marriage and motherhood; the revaluation and re-entering of motherhood; and the possibility that woman can be economically and emotionally independent.

Efuru, in *Efuru* sets a feminist example through her longing for independence and as a symbol of survival of legacy of colonialism. She is successful, gay, and liberal, liberated from the bonds of repression and oppression from her first husband Adizua and also from equally carefree and disappointing second husband, Gilbert. Both men symbolize colonial power. But Adizua is benefitted in marrying Efuru without dowry while Gilbert by his Christian name and ideals could marry Efuru. Though Efuru liked freedom most, she also followed traditional practices, such as circumcision, polygamy, traditional beliefs and traditional attitude towards wifehood and infertility. She considers kitchen to be her forte, symbolizing a place of empowerment and weaponry in the truest sense of the term.

Efuru first meets Adizua in a festival where young men and women look for their spouses. Adizua is fascinated by the beauty of Efuru and declares that he would marry her. She too readily agrees to the proposal. They love each other so intensely that Efuru tells Adizua that she would drown herself in the lake if he would deceive her. So also to ensure about his love, Adizua tells that even the dust she trod on is most dear to him. Though he is madly in love with her, he has no money to pay towards the bride price. Both agree to elope on Nkwo day, a market day when people are out of the village. Adizua's mother after returning from the market is shocked to find Efuru with all her belongings in her house.

Adizua convinced his mother that he could marry her without paying bride price. His mother felt elated for her son's choice and started showering love upon Efuru and treating her like her own daughter. Efuru's father was enraged when he heard about her elopement with Adizua and deputed some elders of his clan to get her back. Efuru offered them Kola nut and gin and assured them that she would never bring shame to her family. Knowing pretty well her husband's economic status, she promised that she would return to her father after sometime along with her husband to pay the bride price. And the elders appreciated her for her courage and conviction for upholding the tradition.

Efuru's father later decided to send another batch of elders to persuade Efuru to get back but to no avail. Finally he severed his relations with his daughter. On the domestic front, when Adizua asked Efuru to work in the farm along with him, the feminist in her bluntly turned down his proposal and declared that she was not cut out for a farm but for trade. She stayed back in the town and started trading. Adizua could not concentrate on his farm and used to frequent town. However, both could save from their earnings the amount required for the bride price to get the legal sanction for their marriage.

Efuru did not conceive for a long time, which caused anxiety in her mother-in-law. When she pleaded with Efuru to get a second wife for his son, Efuru consented to get a second wife for her husband but without sacrificing her position as first wife. But unfortunately, Adizua developed an illicit relationship with Nykoyne. Meanwhile, Efuru conceived and delivered a child who was later named Ogonim. She even employed Ogea, a maidservant, to look after her child. However, her happiness was short-lived as the child died after a brief illness. Adizua, though informed about the death of his child, did not attend the funeral. Efuru, deeply hurt by the indifference of her husband, returned to her father's house once for all and decided to lead life independently.

When Ogea too was taken away by her parents, Efuru found herself lonely and depressed. Later she would meet Enerbi Gilbert, her childhood friend and they talked of their old experiences and gradually their love developed and they married. They were happy for sometime. Again she was destined to suffer as she failed to conceive. Her mother-in-law, dissatisfied with her infertility, compelled Gilbert to go for a second wife. However, when Gilbert too like Adizua failed to attend the funeral of her father, Efuru decided to divorce Gilbert.

Efuru (1966) presents a long awaited departure from the stereotyped female figure in male-authored African fiction. The dynamic Efuru chooses her own man and marries him without his paying a bride price. She is radical in her thinking unlike traditional African woman. When Adizua fails to pay the bride price, she tells him not to bother about it. And they proclaim themselves as married against the norms of society. Efuru unlike traditional woman refuses to work in the farm with her husband. She rightly claims: "I am not cut for farm work. I am going to trade. . . . I want to be nurtured and sustained by the strengths of my culture but I am also prepared to make changes if and when the need arises."[11]

Efuru is a woman struggling hard for recognition and to establish her individual social status in the society. She is portrayed as a promising woman advancing from the beginning of her life till the end encountering many challenges in life but keeping the tradition of marriage and family life. Facing boldly her misfortunes she feels that she has the blessings of Uhamiri, the goddess of the lake. The story of Efuru reveals the author's intention to create a free-spirited, self-reliant, strong-willed and hardworking independent woman. She questions the very traditions in the society and the importance given to men and sympathizes with the plight of women folk unable to raise their voice against the excesses of men.

Stratton has wrongly diagnosed the rebellious nature of Efuru when he says that Efuru's first decision to marry a poor farmer without obtaining her father's consent and even without the bride price being paid to him before the marriage seems to flout the patriarchal authority. Efuru is more a reformer than a rebel, an agent looking forward to and welcoming change to her advantage and other women in the society. She openly confesses that,

> Tell my father that I shall be the last person to bring shame on him since my mother died five years ago, I have been a good daughter to him. My husband is not rich. In fact he is poor. But the dowry must be paid. I must see that this is done. (*Ibid.*)

Efuru negotiates with all the possibilities made available to her. When Adizua desires to marry a second time, she approves wholeheartedly his proposal but on the condition that she retains her status as first wife:

> What is wrong in his marrying a second time? It is only a bad woman who wants her husband all to herself. I don't object to his marrying a second wife but I do object to being relegated to the background. I want to keep my position, as the first wife for it is my right. (62-63)

When Efuru's father pities her marital relationship with Adizua and desires to take her home, she refuses to go with him and says, "I have not made up my mind. Once it is made up there is no coming back." (95)

Efuru as a revolutionary goes beyond the societal norms. She being a staunch feminist divorces her first husband, Adizua and marries Gilbert, her schoolmate. But when Gilbert fails to attend her father's funeral, she even divorces him. She herself is the master of her destiny and the master of her own will.

In her second novel *Idu*, Nwapa emerges as a revisionist who holds man responsible for infertility in woman. Idu rejects the cultural ethics of wife inheritance, male dominance and primacy of the child. Nwapa seems to correct the perceptions of male about women's wants and needs, from the female point of view. Nwapa asserts that the so-called passive, passionless, unimaginative, powerless and irresponsible African woman is a figment of the male's imagination that she has set out to correct. Her fiction provides glimpses of women achieving economic power and exalted positions through participation in religious, business and political activities.

Idu as the most affectionate and devout wife served Adiwere in his sickness. She did not conceive and shared her sorrow with her friend Ojiugo who was also barren. Though Adiwere had a second wife, he continued to love Idu as before. Ewuu, his second wife was quarrelsome and deserted him to marry another man.

Meanwhile, Idu delivered a child and thanked God for blessing her. But people thought the child born on inauspicious day would devour his father. And as suspected Adiewere fell seriously ill and died. Adiewere and Idu after marriage had planned to construct their house and lead happy life but it remained an unfulfilled dream with the sudden death of Adiewere. After twenty-eight days, Idu also died and it was believed that she had joined her husband as devout wife in the next world.

Nwapa in *Idu* writes about the marginality and misrepresentation of women by subtly saying that a woman is not an inanimate object without brains, feelings, emotions and desires. Idu stands for industry, ingenuity and resilience. The novel ends catastrophically with the suicide of an impotent man and a pregnant woman. Childlessness is the main theme interrelating life and death, birth and madness. Women's speeches are sprinkled with anecdotes, oral as well as folk wisdom, moral judgments and sympathy.

Idu is a total contrast to Efuru. Efuru represents a woman of protest whereas Idu signifies submission. Both allow their husbands to go for a second marriage. Efuru asserts her position as first wife but Idu shows much patience and compromises with life. Adiewere, husband of Idu, returns home after becoming sick and Idu nurses him until his last and dies twenty-seven days after his death.

In Nwapa's third novel *One is Enough* Amaka is shocked to learn about her husband, Obioro's illicit relations with other women and is utterly disillusioned. For many days, she suffers the tyranny of her husband as she fails to conceive. Her sensitivity about her barrenness initially subdues her to her husband's violence. But when she is cornered in the bathroom and attacked by her husband, Amaka becomes conscious of her victimization and becomes vengeful. Fearing that Obiora might become too violent, she seeks to protect herself by locking up the bathroom door from inside. When Obiora breaks open the bathroom door, she hits him on the chest with a hammer. This violence provoked by her husband forces Amaka to question her own values and her societal role. She declares that she has desired a man who is not only independent but also pure and simple. She wants a man, not a husband and she would like to be neither a wife nor married. Amaka revolts against female suppression and tells of her desire to assert herself: "As a wife, I am never free. I am a shadow of myself. There is something in that world that doesn't suit me. . . . I am in prison, unable to advance in body and soul. Something gets hold of me as a wife and destroys me."[12]

Amaka becomes the mouthpiece of Flora Nwapa in expounding feminism. She sets an example of a rebel countering man's undue authority and atrocities. Nwapa presents Amaka as a symbol of woman's struggle for a possible way out. Nwapa upholding the innate desire and potentialities in woman seems to be encouraging in *One is Enough* the emergence of 'new' African woman.

Emecheta's works too have portrayed African woman, primarily in the image of mother in Nigerian Society. She has also highlighted how sexuality and the ability to conceive alone sometimes define feminity and womanhood. She represents three societies—Igbo, Yoruba and British. Like Toni Morrison, she believes, "Fiction has a vital social responsibility." The stories she narrates in her novels are entertaining and didactic with message to her readers.

Her first two novels *In the Ditch* and *Second Class Citizen* are autobiographical. And others are paradoxical to her experiences. In 1978, she won the Jock Campbell prize for her novel *The Slave Girl* (1977). In 1979 she won the award for 'the best black writer in Britain' for her novel *The Joys of Motherhood* (1979). Emecheta, branded by her critics as a feminist, sought cooperation from women in America and also from men in Africa to improve the social status and economic condition of black woman:

> I did not start as a feminist. I do not think I am one now. Most of my readers would take this to be the statement of a coward. But it is not. I thought before I would like to be one but after my recent visit to the United States when I talk to real Feminists with a capital F, I think we women of African background still have a very very long way to go before we can really rub shoulders with such men. . .so my sisters in America I am not shunning your advanced help, in fact I still think women of Africa need your contribution and at the same time we need our men.[13]

Alice Walker has observed that Buchi Emecheta "integrates the profession of writer into cultural concepts of mother/worker because she is both." Emecheta is totally committed to the cause of black women. She states, "I have the courage to say I write for blacks." (*Ibid.*)

She has given women positive roles to her women and has also encouraged woman education, which she thinks would advance their position in society. She says that women are capable of living for so many other reasons. She believes that her story with a deep sense of commitment would certainly bring success. About her own commitment she said: "I work towards the liberation of women but I am not a feminist, I am just a woman. Just keep trying and trying. If you have the determination and commitment, you will succeed." (*Ibid.*) Buchi Emecheta believes in her brand of African feminism:

> I do believe in the African kind of feminism. They call it womanism, because you see, you Europeans don't worry about water, you

> don't worry about schooling, you are so well off. Now, I buy land, and I say, 'OK, I can't build on it, I have no money, so I give it to some women to start planting. That is my brand of feminism. (*Ibid.*)

But Emecheta's contemporary, Catherine Acholonu resented Emecheta's brand of feminism. She holds that for Emecheta, individual freedom is but sexual freedom and sexual freedom is tantamount to promiscuity and that many of her female readers would argue against her generalizations on marriage, and on promiscuity as a way out for emancipation of women born of hatred towards men. Buchi Emecheta has also been criticized by some male African writers for her feministic views and called her "hostile emigrant contaminated by European views."

In *The Joys of Motherhood*, Nnu Ego and her husband Nnaife renounce everything to educate first their eldest son Oshia, and then they think of educating their second son Adim, with the left over money. But they never think of educating their daughters. The parents treat daughters only as commodities who would bring in good bride price to invest further on the study of their brothers. Nnu Ego's expectation that her sons would return home to take care of her goes wrong and this she realizes much later. Nnu Ego realized that part of the pride of motherhood was to look a little unfashionable and be able to draw with joy. She could not afford another outfit because she was nursing him. So she could not go anywhere to sell anything. However, Nnu Ego is hopeful that her old age would be comfortable as he would grow soon and clothe her and farm for her, so that her old age would be sweet.

Tsitsi's *Nervous Conditions* also deals with the theme of gender discrimination. As in *The Joys of Motherhood*, it records the bitter experiences of women in general and their craving for independence and equality. Nhamo, the only son in the family, is given education. But unexpectedly he dies leaving the responsibility of the family to Tamboo, the eldest daughter in the family. Even though she is prepared to sustain them, the elders do not accept her offer to help her family in a positive sense. Instead, they find fault with her education saying that she is helping out her husband's family and not her own family.

In her interview with James, Buchi Emecheta speaks of the significant role of women as the guardians of culture. She discussed that idea in her latest book, *The Rape of Shavi* which is about the rape of a culture. At the end of that rape we find it is women who bring things together. Whereas if they had allowed women to take part all along, maybe the rape would not have taken place.

Emecheta confirms that African writers need to become concerned about several other matters other than colonialism and cultural cringe. She says that African literature is deeply concerned about colonialism and the impact of the West on Africa. African writers today write about the human predicament in Africa resulting from years of denigration. Emecheta, though she lives in England, is sentimentally attached to Nigeria and is concerned about the human condition in her homeland.

She feels that Nigeria and African women in general need to bind together to support each other instead of bitching about each other. She is frank enough to declare that in Nigeria women are riddled with hypocrisy. They learn to say what they don't feel. They learn to laugh or not to laugh too loudly.

Her frankness about Nigeria often invites criticism from Nigerian writers who charged that she subjected herself to alien influence sacrificing her African identity. However Emecheta defended herself saying that many African writers strive for recognition outside Africa. Africans are fond of reading cheap American novels than novels by African writers, which in turn has necessitated the African writers to move to Europe for their career receives due encouragement.

Writing about women Emecheta wonders: why women are as they are? Why are they so pathetic? When you hear about traditional women who were very strong, you wonder why we are today so pathetic, so hypocritical. *The Joys of Motherhood* ends with a note: "Nnu Ego had it all yet still did not answer prayers for children."

Nnu Ego in her prayer asks God when He would create a woman with fulfillment as a complete human being and not as anybody's appendage. When talking to Ubani, Nnu Ego says that the money may be small and the work like slave labour, but at least his wife's mind is at rest knowing that at the end of the month she gets some money to feed her children and him. She asks what more a woman wants.

And we approve of Nnu Ego's belief in her fulfillment as woman. Her attitude towards change strains her familiar relationship. She is a slave owned by her husband. But she faces the world boldly as a feminist. Nnu Ego, condemned by the society as an unsuccessful mother, revolts against society for the injustice done to her and justifies her stand.

> She had been brought up to believe that children made a woman. She had had children, nine in all, luckily seven were alive, much more than many women of her period could boast of . . . still, how was she to know that by the time her children grew up the values of her country, her people and her tribe would have changed so drastically, to the extent where a woman with many children could face a lonely old age, and may be a miserable death all alone, just like a barren woman.[14]

The tragedy of Nnu Ego goes beyond her death to suggest that Emecheta is critical also about the behaviour of her protagonist. Emecheta does not remain a silent observer. She seems to suggest remedial solution to Nnu Ego's problem by which she would have been more comfortable in life. Nnu Ego who is portrayed as a traditional and submissive woman accepting all the norms of the society, becomes rebellious against the social conventions.

Buchi Emecheta's poetic rendition *Wives at War* has earned her reputation as Africa's most sustained and vigorous feminist voice of protest. *In the Ditch* (1972) is Emecheta's autobiographical novel written after divorcing her husband. The main focus of the novel is on the importance of initiation and determination of Adah to revolt against the norms and customs of the society, an attempt to get out of the ditch.

Second Class Citizen (1974) is her second novel depicting the frustration and distress experienced by a young foreign mother in a strange and inhospitable country. The basic theme of the novel is hatred towards gender discrimination. *The Joys of Motherhood* (1979) also known as *The Mother, The Mother's Mother, The Mother's Early Life* and *First Shock of Motherhood* is acknowledged as the most successful and realistic African novel. She narrates the agony Nnu Ego underwent in the male chauvinistic society.

She describes the hardships and problems faced by an immigrant living by herself unsupported by male. The story is about a young mother's concern for her children. She tries to provide all comforts to them in a patriarchal polygamous society. The novel also explores the ethical problems of a poor family. The lives of two women Adaku and Nnu Ego mark the difference between realism and illusion, between sanity and lunacy.

The Joys of Motherhood is a study of victimization and enslavement of a traditional Igbo woman to the dictates of Igbo culture. The novel reflects the different stances of motherhood with their consequences. As a feminist she speaks out against imperialism, "I don't know if death isn't better than this! There is nothing we can do. The British own us just like God does, and just like God they are free to take any of us when they wish." (147-48)

When Nnu Ego is forced to rear her children she bluntly argues, "As for my daughters, they will have to take their own chances in the world. I am not prepared to stay here to be the mad woman, just because I have no son." (169-70) Nnu Ego's anguish over the possible death of herself speaks of the tyranny of the British imperialism. The novelist is critical of the protagonist for her indignity and lack of aspirations. Nnu Ego dies a miserable death by the roadside thinking that she has reached her home. She dies quietly with no child, no friend to talk to her. She has never really made friends with anybody as she has kept herself very busy as a true mother taking utmost care of her children. But she dies in the end as a destitute.

Emecheta's novel *The Bride Price* (1976) depicts how an African woman becomes a scapegoat and allows herself to be sold as a commodity for good bride price. "People adhere to the belief that a female is worthless to a family except for the bride price she will bring to it."[15]

The novel speaks of the African age-old customs, female suppression and sexism. Aku-nna and Nna-nndo live with their father Ezekiel Odio, often called Nna in Lagos. Aku-nna is thirteen-year-old taking after her father in stature and nature as she is fondly called Aku-nna, which means father's wealth. Her father is anxious to get big bride price for her when she would get married to a wealthy man. He works as a head-moulder at the Loco yard in Lagos. One day he hurts his leg and gets hospitalized for treatment. When he does not return home, Aku-nna becomes anxious and is consoled by her uncle Joseph and Uche.

The next day when the dead body of her father is brought home, Aku-nna and Nna-nndo are shocked by the sudden demise of their father. Her mother Ma Blackie returns to Lagos to bring her children back to Ibuza. The people of Lagos bid farewell to the family with little presents and tears. But Aku-nna desires to marry a person hailing from Lagos and not from Ibuza. Further, when the family moves to her father's brother, Okonkwo's house, her mother is compelled to become his fourth wife.

Okonkwo gets Aku-nna married to Okoboshi, a physically challenged person for a big bride price. Aku-nna unwillingly marries him as she has already given her heart to Chike. On the very first day after her marriage, she rebukes Okoboshi and runs away with Chike. Chike following the tradition pays more bride price to Okonkwo to own Aku-nna. Aku-nna gets her brother educated with the help of her husband. She delivers a child and names it as 'Joy' to symbolize her unfulfilled joy and dies after few days.

> So it was that Chike and Akku-nna substantiated the traditional superstition they had unknowingly set out to eradicate. Every girl born in Ibuza after Aku-nna's death was told her story to reinforce the old taboos of the land. If a girl wished to live long and see her children's children, she must accept the husband chosen for her by her people and the bride price must be paid. If the bride price were

> not paid, she would never survive the birth of her first child. It was a psychological hold that existed for a very long time. (176-77)

Buchi Emecheta's novel *The Slave Girl* deals with the change taking place in the country from the colonial period to the period of independence, in fictional terms. In the novel, Ojebeta is portrayed as an assertive woman enjoying social status in the colonial world. *Destination Biafra* (1994) throws light on the horrible things witnessed during the civil war that erupted in the late 1960s in Biafra and the conflicting feelings of Debbi Ogedembge, the Oxford-educated daughter of a corrupt government minister. It is about the active participation of the protagonist in the Biafra's struggle, and the attempt made to bridge the gap between the old and the new and for solidarity between male and female, in Biafra.

Head Above Water is Emecheta's autobiographical novel showing the transformation of Emecheta from a tribal child in African bush to a life in the north of London as an internationally acclaimed writer. She says that as her survival for the past twenty five years in England from which when she was a little over twenty dragging four cold and dripping babies with her and pregnant with the one that was a miracle. And if for any reason we do not believe in miracles, we are requested to start believing, because keeping her head above water in this indifferent society is a miracle.

Kehinde (1994), the latest novel of Emecheta centering on the awareness of cultural priorities and discriminations, presents Kehinde as a Nigerian woman reposing too much of confidence in her husband. She dreams of leading a happy life with her husband Albert. But to her utter disappointment, he returns to Nigeria with a second wife. This transforms Kehinde into a rebel from an affectionate wife and she decides to depart to London against the Nigerian custom. The novel has also recorded Emecheta's own experience at the psychiatric hospital in London where out of eleven patients nine are black, that suffer not from mental illness but because: "that they heard voices and spoke to that voice."[16]

Ama Ata Aidoo, the multifaceted scholar, revolutionary and an exciting writer in literary circles had formal education as a means to mitigate the suffering caused by gender inferiority. She represents women writers in general though she is deeply concerned about lesbianism in African society. As an idealist she has positive attitude towards womanhood. She always scorns male linguistic chauvinism and wants to bring in woman political awareness, and exhibits woman sensitivity to social issues, and her vulnerability to mental stress and physical suffering. She refuses to see her heroines suffering and become victims of circumstances. She too as a feminist gives a feminine perspective of African society.

Aidoo is a bilingual and has acquired fluency in French and developed a fascination for English dramas. Owing to economic constraints, she could not establish a theatre for English drama. As a feminist, she wished to see dramas where women played their prominent roles, in a positive way for bettering the condition of African women in the male-dominated society. Being a black woman, she has admitted her difficulty in understanding the situation in America where people are carefree and irresponsible. She is very pragmatic in her outlook. She liked to write in her stories about lovers in Paris and in other works about sophistication in politics in Africa. She hesitates to use the term 'black power' and call the black American black Negro.

Ama Ata Aidoo produced two dramas and wrote an article entitled "The New African." She held the view that poetry should conform to certain accepted western standards. She opposed western notion of African primitiveness. She liked to read Achebe's *Things Fall Apart* and Shakespeare's *Hamlet* for their commitment to regenerate the society and dealing with universal values.

Our Sister Killjoy or Reflections from a Black-Eyed Squint (1979) is Ama Ata Aidoo's most exciting novel. It is the historically established and culturally sanctioned sexism of African society in terms of lesbianism. Aidoo's character Sissie is an independent, and assertive woman without the support of men. Aidoo in the novel is not interested in bridging the gap between western and African thought but tries to create something novel, different from black or female concerns. Owusu thinks that Aidoo's work. "gives a sense of structural and linguistic irony which is functional. . .signifying a couple of things the need for and very process of revamping."[17]

Changes: A Love Story (1991), Aidoo's most privileged novel, brings political awareness among women. The women like Esi Kom and the grandmother Nana in the novel assert themselves in the patriarchal Akan society. The relationship between these women reflects political suppression experienced by successive generations in the Yawson clan. The repentance and the reconciliation of Esi Kom and Eulalie reflect the existing Diaspora that Aidoo calls Africa's 'amnesia' relating to the slave trade. Eulalie, though presented as a submissive character in the beginning, later becomes a dictator finding a significant position among the women of her community.

But Esi Kom, the protagonist symbolizing modern African women and holding a high position, leads an independent life with her husband and child. She is dissatisfied with her mother and grandmother who have different perception of marriage. Despite their warnings, she separates herself from her husband Oko and prefers to settle down as a second wife to her lover Ali Kondey. Both her mother and grandmother discourage Esi from becoming the second wife of Ali Kondey. But Esi gives a deaf ear to what they have said and lamented.

> She could never be as close to her mother as her mother was to her grandmother. . .why had they sent her to school. . .with no hope of ever meaningfully reentering her mother's world . . . all this was too high a price to pay to achieve the dangerous confusion she was now in and the country was now in.[18]

Esi's economic independence threw her into a confused state of mind regarding the choice of the values of her own culture. Esi complains against her parents for sending her to school for no purpose. Rhetorically she questions her gender discrimination. She has protested saying:

> Why had they sent her to school?
> What had they hoped to gain from it?

> What had they hoped she would gain from it?
> Who had designed the educational system that had produced her sort?
> What had that person or persons hoped to gain from it?[19]

Educated women have to pay a high price resulting in confusion and depriving them of their socio-political rights. Esi's failure to comply with the traditions and remain a faithful granddaughter makes her become philosophical.

Changes: A Love Story presents a young woman as a symbol of African woman's pre-colonial protest, and successfully projects the complexities of colonial political dispensation. Aidoo also presents in the woman's resistance to the political order the contradictions of African women of 1980s and 1990s. The writer by glorifying the African past makes the woman become nostalgic about her pre-colonial position.

Aidoo also presents the intricacies of the conflict in terms of modernity reflected in African woman and society and the conflict between the age-old traditions and their aspirations to ignore them. Aidoo is satirical about the attitude of modern women in African context. Modern Ghanaian women too experience similar predicament and problems hindering their progress in their life.

Changes is the story of a woman trying to discover herself and her futile attempt to strike a balance between her desire for freedom and her craving for love and recognition within the Ghanaian culture. And she finds Ghanaian culture very accommodative. It focuses on how modern African women like Esi Sekyi, Opokuya Dakwa and Fusena Kondey view their lives and the strategies they adopt for self-improvement encountering the challenges of postcolonial African society on all fronts. They face many problems to marry grooms of their choice. As educated African women, they are in a dilemma whether to go by social convention or against the tradition because of the reaction to their thinking within the family and society. Esi is rebellious in nature, while Opokuya and Fusena decide to lead traditional married life.

The Dilemma of the Ghost (1965) focuses on the placement of women in West African communities. It speaks of familial relationship between mother and daughter which later turns into the relation between mother and daughter-in-law. Aidoo presents a promising picture of a woman involved in political activities of her male dominated Akan society. *Anowa* succeeds in replacing Eurocentric feminist bias in historical context. Living in a matriarchal society, Aidoo upholds the status of women: "Women were everything: they were supposed to hold the power . . . yet when a priestess had her period she couldn't approach her own shrine."[20]

Ama Ata Aidoo's *Our Sister Killjoy* narrates a traveller's tale like Joseph Conrad's *Heart of Darkness.* Sissie is a member of the Ghanaian branch of INVOLOU, of the voluntary organization popularly called VOLOU. Sissie represents a section of the black women which indulges in debauchery and selfish and indifferent to the order and harmony in society and giving itself sentimentally to European values without properly understanding social morality and human virtues. Sissie returns to Africa unscathed as she has shown restraint in not becoming a lesbian attracted towards her German friend, Marija.

Aidoo makes Sissie conduct her journey not into the territories of darkness in *Heart of Darkness* but into the human landscapes of civilization. Her departure from the Ghanaian airport is a retelling of the myth of conceptual polarities, as presented in a morality play by Africans and Europeans to represent savagery and civilization, respectively.

Marija's village has a castle turned into a hostel for the young volunteers from abroad. In that castle it is said once lived a lord controlling the destiny of many serfs. For Marija, Sissie is but a sexual object like Kurtz's savage Amazon in Conrad's *Heart of Darkness.* Aidoo, in Sissie has evoked a debased black woman as in colonial fiction. The relationship between Sissie and Marija, with cultural angularities, reflects the sterility of European civilization and European's facile assumptions about morality. As Kwaku Larbi Korang observes, the fundamental asymmetry of power coincides with Sissie and Marija's racial locations, and displaces the notion of a Catholic feminity and universal humanity as meaningful political possibilities for Aidoo's novel. In fact Aidoo uses their friendship to warn Africa of the serious consequences of her total dependency on Europe.

Aidoo like her male Ghanaian counterpart, Ayi Kwei Armah, says that they [Africans] have been so long following the falling sun, flowing to the desert, moving to their burial. Africa's dependency on Europe is suicide, and suicide, they know, is murder with the consent of victim. Sissie leaves Germany to visit her African 'brothers' in London, who continue to stay on even after the completion of their studies, to tell them that they are addicted to the poison that would kill them. It is time for them to decolonize their minds, to go back to Africa and contribute to its development.

The female Nigerian critic Chikwenye Okonjo Ogunyemi has made her own assessment about the two feminist writers, "If Nwapa is the challenger, Buchi Emecheta is the fighter . . . for the first time, female readers through female characters are aware of their subjugation by their fathers, uncles, husbands, brothers and sons."[21]

Nwapa's work is a biography, a collective biography of beautiful, strong Ugwuta women and about their majestic lake capturing the complexities, ambiguities and contradictions of their environment as embodied in the force that lies at the bottom of the lake. Flora Nwapa openly confesses that she is not a feminist, but an ordinary woman projecting the images of women positively. She has also admitted that she is just an ordinary writer, who as a sensitive committed writer has to write about her women folk. Like several other writers, she too is expressive and communicative with a social purpose.

> I have tried several times to take university appointments and work as a critic but each time I have packed up and left without giving notice. I found that I could not bring myself to criticize other people's work. . .for myself I don't deal with great ideological issues. I write about the little happenings of everyday life. Being a woman and African born, I see things through an African woman's eyes. I chronicle the little happenings in the lives of the African women I know. I did not know that by doing so I was going to be called a

> feminist. But if I am now a feminist then I am an African feminist with a small 'f'.[22]

But unlike other African writers, Nwapa expects a woman to be dynamic and to oppose tradition where necessary for her advancement. She has cautioned women: "a woman who holds her husband as a father dies an orphan."[23] To her, a woman should be economically independent, not relying on inheritance or on men for survival. Buchi Emecheta, an immigrant of Nigeria, insists on following family tradition and works for the well-being of their family.

Buchi Emecheta, Mariama Ba and Flora Nwapa belong to the second generation of African women writers in presenting women as complex characters radical in their attitude symbolizing modern feminism. Emecheta's novel *The Joys of Motherhood*, which is ironically titled, exposes the sufferings of Nnu Ego resulting from motherhood. There is a striking similarity between Nwapa's Efuru and Emecheta's Nnu Ego. Both have lost their mothers before the novel begins and are victims of patriarchy.

Both get married twice and lead a miserable life. Efuru did not conceive for a long time while Nnu Ego suffered as her sons neglected her. But the basic difference between the two characters is that Nnu Ego's husband divorces her for infertility while Efuru, though infertile, divorces her husband allowing him to opt for a second wife. Nnu Ego bears the insult and sees herself as a failure. She confesses, "I am sure the fault is on my side. How can I face my father and tell him that I have failed." (31)

Efuru refuses to accept her infertility and claims her original position even after her husband marries a second time. She bluntly argues, "I want to keep my position, as the first wife for it is my right." (63) Emecheta's Adaku, the co-wife of Nnu Ego and Nwapa's Efuru resemble each other. Adaku is also hardworking, strong-willed trader with a great sense of freedom. But unlike Efuru, she is blessed with children mostly girls born to others. While Adaku enjoys little respect, Efuru is praised for her sacrificing nature.

Flora Nwapa and Ama Ata Aidoo present a different picture of the role of African woman representing her generation and not compromising with the political change. Nwapa's novels are set in urban areas. The chief concern of Nwapa's novels is woman's barrenness whereas Aidoo's novels deal with other problems of African women than infertility. Nwapa's novels focus on the deity 'Chi' as the most powerful mother of Ugwutha community. Aidoo does not present African society as highly superstitious. Nwapa's women try to become economically independent while Aidoo's women occupy significant positions in society.

Emecheta has proclaimed that she does not sympathize with a woman who deserts her children and with a woman who would stay with a brute as husband only to be regarded in society. She says that she has no sympathy for a woman who deserts her children; neither does she have sympathy for a woman who insists on staying in a marriage with a brute of a man simply to be respectable.

All the novels of Emecheta expound, "the theme of female oppression, the slave girl becoming her leit motif-the archetypal African woman buried alive under the heavy yoke of traditional mores and customs."[24] Virginia Woolf observes:

> Saadawi's *Women at Point Zero*, Flora Nwapa's *Efuru* and *One is Enough*, Buchi Emecheta's *Second Class Citizen*, *The Slave Girl* and *Joys of Motherhood* are all united by their possession of respective maladies: They are blessed with all the features of fairy tales and myth; they unabashedly distort with indecency and uncanny bravado history, sociology and gender images just to make some shallow feminist point; their heroines are conveniently spared healthy competitions as they only thrive in outlandish communities peopled by only weak., emasculated, lazy, foolish and insane men.[25]

Achebe's Okonkwo is obstinate, violent and arrogant like Nnu Ego of Buchi Emecheta's *Joys of Motherhood.* Buchi Emecheta protests against the victimization of women in Igbo society and she converts personal problems into a public crusade only to expose the society. Buchi too, like Chinua Achebe, does not merely expose the society of its evils and social injustices, but also highlights the good of native tradition. Achebe has portrayed women characters as highly submissive, obedient to their husbands and abiding by the customs and traditions of Igbo society. But the women in the novels of Achebe lack depth. Except sexual subjugation, the real affinity that strengthens the bonds of marital relationship is lacking in his novels whereas women are powerful and independent with individuality in the works of Flora Nwapa. They demand love and affection and their rightful place in society and family as wife.

Only in *Anthills of the Savannah* Achebe has portrayed Beatrice as an intellectual and a journalist who has advanced in the Nigerian contemporary society. The Igbo traditional society in Achebe's novels seems to be governed by the female principle. It is Ani, the goddess of Earth that controls the social morality. The crises—social, political and cultural—emerged with the arrival of the white man. There were events in Igbo land when women supported their men in resisting the entry of the British. Women too became concerned about the political change in Igbo land.

Toni Morrison has observed that Achebe's female characters are without male-bias. With Achebe she never felt the male claw grabbing up the entire canvas; there was feminine space where women existed without permission from the man. Like Toni Morrison, Emecheta too believes in functional fiction: "Fiction has a vital social responsibility."

Both deal with women's problems and prejudices against women in the black African society. Buchi Emecheta as a womanist is interested in the positive portrayals of women. Ogunyemi has pointed out that womanism in Africa is but a celebration of black roots and womanism is a philosophy that celebrates black roots, the ideas of black life, while giving a balanced presentation of black womandom.

NOTES

1. Jone Johnson Lewis, *Wisdom Quotes: Quotations to Inspire and Challenge.*
2. *Ibid.*
3. *Ibid.*

4. *Ibid.*
5. Annual Report by UNAIDS and WHO—Reuters, London 23.11.04
6. Sharon Verba, *Feminist and Womanist Criticism of African Literature: A Bibliography*: July 20, 1997.
7. *America's Working Women:* A Documentary History, 1600 to the Present rev. and updated ed. 1993.
8. *Imperial Leather: Race, Gender, Sexuality in the Colonial Context* (New York: Routledge, 1995).
9. Flora Nwapa's Interview with Dr. Akachi Ezeigbo, *Independent Weekly*, 22-28 August, 1993.
10. Flora Nwapa, *One is Enough* (London: Heinemann, 1981), p. 22.
11. Flora Nwapa, *Efuru* (London: Heinemann, 1966), p. 5.
12. *One is Enough*, p. 127.
13. Umeh Marie, *Emerging Perspectives on Buchi Emecheta* (Trenton: NJ: Africa World, 1996).
14. Buchi Emecheta, *The Joys of Motherhood* (New York: George Brazillier, 1979), p. 219.
15. Buchi Emecheta, *The Bride Price* (New York: George Braziller, 1976), p. 10.
16. Buchi Emecheta's interview with Julie Holmes, *The Voice*, July 9, 1966.
17. Kofi Owusu, "*Canons under Siege: Blackness, Femaleness and Ama Ata Aidoo's Our Sister Killjoy*" (Callaloo, 1990).
18. Ama Ata Aidoo, *Changes* (Tana, Enugu, 1981).
19. Aidoo, *Changes: A Love Story* (London: Women's Press, 1991).
20. Aidoo, "Literature, Feminism and the African Woman Today" African Literature Association Conference, Stony Brook, New York, March, 1996.
21. Chikwenyeokonjo Ogunyemi, "Women and Nigerian Literature: Perspectives on Nigerian Literature, Volume 1. Lagos, Nigeria: Guardian Books, 1988.
22. Interview with Flora Nwapa "The Poetics of Economic Independence for Female Empowerment" by Marie Umeh, *Research in African Literatures*, 1995.
23. Chikwenyeokonjo Ogunyemi, *Women and Nigerian Literature: Perspectives on Nigerian Literature*, Volume 1 (Lagos, Nigeria: George Braziller, 1979).
24. D. Ejinkeonye Ugochukwu, *Discussions on Literary Feminism.* Nigeria, December, 2003.
25. Chikwenyeokojo Ogunyemi, *Women and Nigerian Literature: Perspectives on Nigerian Literature*, Volume1.

Chapter V

Narrative Technique in the West African Novel

Mark Schorer opines that the narrative technique is the mode of existence of the narrator. He says: "When we speak of technique, then we speak of nearly everything. For, technique is the means by which the writer's experience, which is his subject matter, compels him to attend to it. Technique is the only means he has of discovering, exploring, developing his subject, of conveying meaning and finally of evaluating it."[1]

Techniques of narration in fiction pertain to events, occurrences, action, verbal representation and method of story-telling. Following the classification of narrative offered by Gerald Genette, in 1972 Shlomith Rimmon-Kenan discriminated between the elements of narrative history, story, text and narration. Rimmon-Kenan says: "Story designates the narrated events, abstracted from their dispositions in the text and reconstructed in their chronological order, together with the participants in these events . . . whereas story is a succession of events, text is a spoken or written discourse which undertakes their telling."[2]

What is remarkable in the technique of narration is that the narrator at no point withdraws and makes amendments to what he has said. The Joycean ideal of refining the artist out of existence cannot be dramatized by its rhetoric. Technique manipulates the story in the form of direct vision. The artists with a view to narrowing the range of their human enquiry must delimit their stories. The great advantage of the technique in history is that it is vividly portrayed to enable the artist create a world with accepted values and universal experience.

Wayne Booth observes: "The emotions and judgments of the implied author are as I hope to show the very stuff out of which great fiction is made."[3] The African novelist intends to explore the mind and analyze the experiences of his characters in his narrative. His objectivity and discretion, when presented through the technique, are effective and graceful. The rhetoric plays a pivotal role in making the technique more emphatic. Rhetoric in the West African novel is broadly divided into two categories viz., traditional and experimental. Some of the African writers used indigenous techniques of narration, while the modern African writers experimented with the new novelistic modes for effective presentation and to appeal to the outside audience.

The traditional novelist sounds monotonous in his descriptions of 'things' native whereas the modern writer feels like shaking the certitudes. The writer's success lies in his dexterous moulding of the rhetoric to project his vision to give better perspective of his narrative.

The West African novelists exhibit a degree of uncertainty in recording and analyzing personal and collective experiences of Africans in a world that is not wholly African. In incidents of interior monologue, the rhetoric heightens our awareness of idealism. The hero disguises himself and conceals his ideals. The artist uses his characters to explore his own mind. The success of modern artist lies in his ability to share his own experiences with those of his characters to make them real and convincing. The novelists work from a set of accepted norms and ideals and manage to celebrate the events of the past or present with the rhetoric used as a mode for sharing values.

Time becomes the medium of narrative art. The rhythm of the novel essentially is the rhythm of time: events, movements, beginnings, and closures—all the fictional material is compounded by time. The strength of the narrative depends on the artist's mode of presentation of the events in association with other essentials of narrative. These events, though not chronologically significant, remain in the mind of the reader at a point of time. The writers are conscious of time and resent the event in the sequence of time. The treatment of time in literature differs from the logical scientific construct of time. The elements of time like measurement, order, and duration stand as a yardstick for the artist.

The concern for family and native values in the tradition-bound African society is reflected in the change the society is undergoing. Okonkwo in Chinua Achebe's *Things Fall Apart*, popularly called the 'roaring flame,' feels depressed to look at his son, Nwoye who has inherited the qualities of his grandfather, Unoka. Nwoye being lazy, improvident and quite incapable of thinking of tomorrow makes Okonkwo think:

> Perhaps he was not his son. No! He could not be. His wife had played him false. He could teach her! But Nwoye resembled his grandfather, Unoka, who was Okonkwo's father. He pushed the thought out of his mind. He, Okonkwo, was called a flaming fire. How could he have begotten a woman for a son? At Nwoye's age Okonkwo had already become famous throughout Umucfia for his wrestling and his fearlessness. He sighed heavily, and as if in sympathy the smouldering log also sighed and immediately Okonkwo's eyes are opened and he saw the whole matter clearly. Living fire begets cold, impotent ash.[4]

In Flora Nwapa's *Efuru*, when Efuru's daughter Ogonim falls sick, she grows tense and even fears her own possible death.

> "What will I do if I lose her?" she thought. "If she dies, that will mean the end of me." It was then that she remembered what the dibia told her and Adizua when they went to him after the birth of Ogonim. Dibia after breaking the kola saw that something was wrong. He was not sure what it was. He had asked them to come again on Eke day and before that day; they heard that he was dead. "What did he see?" Efuru asked herself. It was only now that Efuru thought seriously of what Dibia told her and her husband more than a year ago. And she was very frightened. . . . She saw herself walking behind her husband with their presents for the dibia on her head. She remembered how the dibia greeted them.[5]

The narrative, with conventional beginnings, operated within a loose temporal and spatial orientation, forms the main mode of narration. The novel with temporal order moulds the consciousness of the readers and the prominence of the intention of the author can be understood from the events selected and their organization in time sequence. The possible apparent ambiguity can be avoided through the idiom of expression. Modern fiction fuses the present with the past to make African fiction most relevant and highly contemporaneous.

Fictional modes like dream, journey as metaphor and flashback also help in plot construction. The first temporal factor in fiction is the artistic blending of dual patterns of narrated time and narrative time. The other aspect of time in a novel is history, the events of the past and is super text, an added dimension of the novel. The implications of the relation between the event and narration would result in the possible interpretative assimilation and evaluation.

Though the novels of Chinua Achebe and Wole Soyinka are primarily social criticism, the writers have employed irony and satire to interest the outsiders. They are a new kind of fiction of the anthropologist and novelist. They are neither novels of history nor pieces of propaganda but works of art in their own right. The African novelists, exploring the human condition, try to analyze African experience and situation in terms of private dream and public concern, in the time sequence and finally experience defined in terms of time becomes the end product of the exposure of narrative.

African novel is not static, a pensive caricature of the past, presented by the novelist. African novelist is also an artist, with a sense of history shaping the destiny of African society. Most of the African writers are fully conscious of their history and use the past in their works. African writers with a deep sense of commitment trace the impact of colonization on the contemporary society and try to relate it to the present.

The writers view the pre-colonial past as a prelude and the colonial past as an interlude, ultimately to culminate in the synthesis of the past and the present to recreate future. In fact, the modern African novel is one of reconciliations, transformations of social selves through the discovery of the essentials of African cultural tradition. Authorial intervention is most common in West African fiction that is highly functional.

In the words of Emmanuel Obiechina, the integrative in which background and atmosphere are interlaced with the action of the narrative must be regarded as Achebe's greatest achievement. Achebe's novel is didactic with profound message and experimental by African expressions and speech rhythms and Pidgin English and by being 'innovative' in the use of native techniques of narration.

Chinua Achebe's rhetoric in the opening page of *Things Fall Apart* establishes the norms to justify the stature of Okonkwo, the protagonist and to localize the principal character, and describe the prowess of Oknokwo by indirectly saying that Oknokwo threw Amalinze, the Cat, a great wrestler of Umuofia. The physical description of Okonkwo in just few words, not giving elaborate descriptions, speaks of Achebe's craftsmanship. To contrast the two—Amalinze and Okonkwo—it is said: "Amalinze was wily craftsman while Oknokwo was as slippery as fish in water." (3)

Achebe has dexterously used proverbs and sayings reflecting ancestral wisdom in the conversations in his narrative. His intention is to capture the dynamic spirit of the Igbo traditional society. Okonkwo is able to recreate a self-enclosed world with norms of glory and self-repentance. *Things Fall Apart* is viewed as an ethnographic document, a study in characterization and for some it is a struggle between modernists who have become loyal to the white man and traditionalists. Because of ethnological details, the novel is viewed as a manifestation of oral literature. Achebe's frequent use of adages, proverbs and African imagery evoke the native ethos in the novel. In the Igbo society it is said that men of title are revered. Elders say: "If a child wash his hands he could eat with kings." (8)

· In Achebe's third novel *The Arrow of God*, the narrator who is an elder of the village Umuaro, begins with Ezeulu's watching the arrival of the new Moon. He tells that the sighting of new Moon is the prerogative of the chief priest who afterwards proclaims the date for the New Yam Festival. The dramatization of action of Ezeulu and spiritualizing of the event make the reader curious about African customs. The chief priest represents the spiritual authority in the African traditional society. But he is exceptional by his queer behavior and eccentricities.

Ezeulu assumes the role of a shepherd protecting his villagers. It is said that when an adult is in the house, the she-goat is not left to suffer the pains of parturition on its tether. Ezeulu becomes mentally derailed when he goes against his village and the will of the chief deity, Ulu. Ezeulu's inordinate ambition to become one of the lords of his village and his queer desire to withhold the date for the New Yam festival and thus not allowing people to harvest their crop, intrude into the domain of Ezeulu. The rhetoric used in the conversation between Ezeulu and Nwaka is quite interesting. The proverbs in the Igbo traditional society, in the words of Achebe, are like palm oil with which words are eaten. The proverbs packed with ancestral wisdom are drawn from oral literature material. Nwaka says that Wisdom is like a goatskin bag, every man carries his own and knowledge of the land is also like that.

Even the dialogues in the narrative are in the form of proverbs. Achebe's novel *Things Fall Apart* abounds in such proverbs.

> A man who pays respect to the great, paves the way for his own greatness. (18)
> The sun will shine on those who stand before it, shines on those who kneel under it. (7)
> A toad does not run in the daytime for nothing. (19)
> Living fire begets cold, impotent ash. (140)

In Buchi Emecheta's *The Slave Girl*, the narrator comments on the unfolding of the events of the story and depicts how miserable Ojebeta's lead ended in great distress. In chapter thirteen, the narrator says in the concluding paragraph: "the irony was that the process would eventually come full circle and people would reject their English names, but that was to be in the days of independence after the end of colonialism. That was in the future."[6] The slave girl is too speculative in chapter fifteen. It never occurred to her that the big house would be sold or that, if she had married Clifford, she might have become a changed person with the different values who would not have felt so alien in a luxurious house.

In Ama Ata Aidoo's *Our Sister Killjoy*, the description of Sissie's voyage to Europe and her experiences are autobiographical. Sissie's inner voice reflects the artist's vision. In fact the modern Sissie's voice mingled with lyrical interludes prove that Ama Ata Aidoo is not just narrating the experience but also revealing it through the subjectivity of Sissie emerging from her own experience.

Oral traditions which include folk tales, proverbs, myths, riddles and local legends, form an integral part of African life and culture and go in the making of African literary tradition. Oral traditions reflect local pride and national interest; the traditional way of life and legends strengthen social life and morality. Legends spread culture and keep the tradition alive. Legendary figures by their accomplishments set models to the society to emulate and some have attained even the status of demi-gods in African mythology. Legendary figures have become a part of history by virtue of their prowess believed to have engaged African spirit beings in a dual battle for weeks. Few Africans of the nineteenth and twentieth centuries who resisted colonial cultural domination and encountered the white administration have become heroes of worship.

African popular folk tales too as part of oral literature are didactic and help in keeping the age-old traditions and practices and the native faith. Folk tales are more familiar and interesting to the native audience than scriptures. African folk tales interest children and younger generation when narrated effectively by their elders highlighting African virtues and strengths of traditional society and especially when accompanied by dramatic and musical performances and when the storytellers inspire them to participate physically and verbally. Riddles of Africa evoke rich African imagery and though sometimes they sound vulgar, they appear to be puzzling by being metaphorical. Riddles sharpen the wisdom and reflect people's basic concerns and interests.

In African traditional society, ceremonies and communal celebrations are meant to cohere people. All participate actively in public celebrations. There is naming ceremony at the time of birth of a child and title-taking ceremony when titles are conferred on individuals in a title-society and second burial ritual on the third day after the death of an individual. Africans involve their neighbours at the time of betrothal and while settling bride price and there is communal 'uni' celebration while sending their daughter to her in-laws.

As per the tradition, the parents of the bride before marriage consult the Oracle of the Hills and the Caves to find out if the marriage would be successful. The entire village participates in the celebration of the marriage and close relations and neighbours decide the bride price to be given to the bride's family. Also the would-be bridegroom presents Kola nuts, alligator pepper to the parents of his bride as a mark of good will. The bride price in the traditional society gets enhanced with the education of a girl. In Buchi Emecheta's *The Bride Price* Aku-nna's father upholds the tradition of the bride price.

> He had named her Aku-nna meaning literally 'father's wealth', knowing that the only consolation he could count on her from her would be her bride price. To him this was something to look forward to. Aku-nna on her part was determined not to let her father down. She was going to marry a rich man of whom her father would approve and who would be able to afford an expensive bride price.[7]

People believe that since she married Chike violating the norms, she died after delivering a child, who was ironically christened Joy. And Aku-nna's death is ascribed to her going against the age-old traditions and the people of Ibuza narrate her story only to emphasise the taboos of the land.

> If a girl wished to live long and see her children's children she must accept the husband chosen for her by her people and the bride price must be paid. If the bride price was not paid, she would never survive the birth of her first child. It was a psychological hold that existed for a very long time.[8]

In African traditional society the kindred after the death of an individual perform on the third day Second Burial ritual inviting the entire village for feast and singing and dancing. But the individual with swelling on body is not given normal burial. He is thrown into the evil forest to die for the community disregards the persons with deformity.

At the time of the Second Burial ceremony of Ezeudu, a great warrior in the village Umuofia, there is much shouting, firing of guns and beating of drums and frenzied dancing. The decision was:

> Ezeudu was to be buried after dark with only a glowing brand to light the sacred ceremony. Darkness was around the corner and the burial was near. Guns fired the last salute and the cannon rent the sky. And then from the centre of the delirious fury came a cry of agony and shouts of horror. It was as if a spell had been cast. All was silent. In the centre of the crowd a boy lay in a pool of blood. It was a dead man's sixteen-year-old son who with his brothers and half brothers had been dancing the traditional farewell to their father. Okonkwo's gun had exploded and a piece of iron had pierced the boy's heart. (30)

African traditional society celebrates public festivals like Pumpkin Leaves Festival, a purification ceremony before the sowing of Yam seed and New Yam Festival before the harvest of Yam seed crop involving the entire village. In *Things Fall Apart*, yam symbolizes masculinity. Okonkwo believes:

> Yam stood for manliness, and he who could feed his family on yams from one harvest to another was a very great man indeed. Okonkwo wanted his son to be a great farmer and a great man. He would stamp out that disquieting sign of laziness, which he thought he already saw in him. (46)

The Umuofians celebrate the New Yam Festival for three days. On the first day it is celebrated with great joy in the household offering sacrifice of new yam and palm oil to their ancestors. On the second day a great wrestling match is held in the village of Okonkwo and on the third day they honour the winners by playing on big drums, singing and dancing.

> Who will wrestle for our village?
> Okafo will wrestle for our village.

Has he thrown a hundred men?
He has thrown four hundred men.
Has he thrown a hundred cats?
He has thrown four hundred cats.
Then send him word to fight for us. (44)

Egungun festival is celebrated in the memory of ancestors. People believe that the spirits of their ancestors in the 'mmo' world still influence their survivors and the community in general. The villagers wearing masks in various forms representing their ancestors perform a ritual dance and in certain communities women also join the dancers.

Witchcraft is part of the accepted supernatural landscape of Africa and the practicing witch doctors are believed to protect the innocent rural folk from evil spirits. They are the privileged class in the traditional society endowed with mystical powers. In *Things Fall Apart*, Okonkwo's wife follows 'Chielo', the priestess of Agbala, the Oracle of the Hills and the Caves, when she takes her daughter Eginma to the shrine of Agbala for the treatment.

> In ordinary life Chielo was a widow with her two children. She was very friendly with Ekwefi and they shared a common shed in the market. She was particularly fond of her daughter Ezinma. Any one seeing Chielo in ordinary life would hardly believe she was the same person who prophesied when the spirit of Agbala was upon her. (44)

African writers have used African imagery for authenticity and characterization and to signify aspects of African cultural tradition. While the red kola nut symbolizes long life, and white kola nut good luck, beer symbolizes friendship. For Africans Ani, the Goddess of earth stands for fertility and sky for fecundating rain, rigidity, fate and death.

NOTES

1. Mark Schorer, *Technique as Discovery: The Theory of the Novel* ed. Philip Stevick (New York: The Free Press, 1967), p. 58.

2. Shlomith Rimmon-Kenan, *Narrative Fiction: Contemporary Poetics*, (New York: Methuen, 1983).
3. Wayne C. Booth, *The Rhetoric of Fiction* (Chicago: The University of Chicago Press, 1961), p. 86.
4. Chinua Achebe, *Things Fall Apart* (London: Heinemann, 1958), p. 140.
5. Flora Nwapa, *Efuru*, (London: Heinemann, 1966) 79.
6. Buchi Emecheta, *The Slave Girl* (New York: George Braziller, 1979), pp. 176-77.
7. Buchi Emecheta, *The Bride Price*, (London: Heinemann, 1976), p. 4.
8. *Things Fall Apart*, pp. 111-12.

Chapter VI

Conclusion

Feminism is a cry against male chauvinism, eternal degradation, constant humiliation, perpetual victimization and inequality in socio-economic and political spheres. It is a voice of the suppressed and oppressed lot struggling to come out of the clutches of the so-called civilized society ill-treating women. It is an attempt to break away from the servitude, insubordination and forceful exploitation of womanhood and an attempt at recognition of woman as equal in all spheres of life.

Most African feminists espouse 'womanism' which Alice Walker defines in restricted sense referring to black womanhood, "as a philosophy that celebrates black roots, the ideals of black life, while giving a balanced presentation of black womanhood . . . its aim is the dynamism of wholeness and self healing." [1]

Akpayom Imoh, a student of Federal Government Secondary School, Nigeria, penned a poem for a school publication. The poem titled: "I Hate Being a Girl" speaks of the deep-rooted bias against female 'race':

> From birth a gift of mixed feeling
> Accepted rather with reluctance
> For the mission she has come to fulfill
> Christened 'father's wealth' 'father's desire'
> A reflection of the role she has come to play
> A mere disquieting thing;
> No matter how loving, good and beautiful
> She can never be initiated
> Into the family circle.[2]

Gina Houng Lee, the Co-coordinator of the Fiji Women's Rights Movement opines that feminism is woman's having control over her own life, how she wants to live her life and make decisions about her own life. Zaynab Alkali, the feminist propagandist has observed, "certain women have used this feminist issue to shout themselves hoarse about certain ideas. Many women use the feminist movement to get back at men. So you have this feminist thing which is one big cover where people give their own interpretation to what it is."[3]

The chief concern of a 'feminist' or 'womanist' is uplift of woman struggling to find her destiny on her own overcoming all the external hurdles and self-imposed inhibitions. It is an attempt to counter her status, emerging from age-old suppression and mute victimization. Feminism aims at transforming the discriminatory attitude of men towards womanliness. More than claiming equal rights in all walks of life on par with men, the activists of feminism feel the need to prevail upon the biased men for better treatment and to consider them richly deserving and equally privileged class in all aspects.

Feminism in African context is no exception to this generalized view. A detailed study of African writings with special reference to West African novel reveals certain factors responsible for the emergence of 'feminism' that are akin to the conducive factors elsewhere across the globe. A close look at the writings of various prominent female writers suggests that all are not alike in their attitude towards presenting the problems of women. As such writers differ from the other in their perception of the problems and in taking them onto the canvas. Their comprehension of the problem varies, though the prevailing atmosphere in the African social set-up is not a significant variant.

In African fiction invariably, the setting is rural and the urban setting focuses the transition affecting African cultural identity. The traditional society has its own social patterns and spiritual processes based on native religion. The behavioural patterns in general are the same or similar in many African societies. People in remote parts of the country hold different views on education, marriage, and employment of women for they are governed by superstitions and traditional beliefs. One who breaks away from the traditional customs and beliefs is viewed as the one possessed by 'Satan' in the Ibo tribe.

Nnaemeka's father in Chinua Achebe's "Marriage is a Private Affair," an extract from his *Girls at War and Other Stories* (1972) says when Nnaemeka refuses to marry the girl whom he had found for him, "I owe it to you, my son, as a duty to show you what is right and what is wrong. Whoever put this idea into your head might as well have cut your throat. It is Satan's work."[4] In traditional society, it is the family and the community that decide the marriage of the individuals. The society has vehemently opposed the church leaders who encouraged education for women. But in urban society, the situation as well as attitude towards women is different.

It is strange to note that the writers, while upholding the traditional and cultural norms, also try to impress their readers with their points of view and progressive ideas. But feminism means different to these writers. Some have blatantly put forth the need to sound feministic while others with an underlying current and the rest with subtle and non-committal tendencies. Some, while focusing the lapse, lay emphasis on the emergence of a new order to redress the endless subservience of woman.

Flora Nwapa, the spokeswoman of 'woman protest' against female suppression and marginalisation of woman is frank enough in spreading feminism in the contemporary African society. She emphasizes on the development of woman through economic independence and self-reliance. Efuru, Idu and Amaka in their own way champion the cause of women. The rebel in them seeks to break the barriers of woman subjugation over the ages. It is also in a way a struggle for self-realization and liberation for economic and personal freedom. There seems to be a quest for emancipation of woman from physical, economic and psychological bondage and to make her more independent and assertive. Flora Nwapa claims:

> I am just an ordinary writer, an ordinary writer who has to write, because if I don't write, I think I would have to be put in an asylum. Some people have to communicate, and I happen to be one of them. I have tried several times to take University appointment

> and work as a critic, but each time I have packed up and left without giving notice. I found that I could not bring myself to criticize other people's work.[5]

Umeh Marie in her interview with Flora Nwapa, elicits the opinion of Nwapa on being called a radical feminist by Frank Katherine in her article, "Women without Men: The Feminist Novel in Africa."

> I don't think I am a radical feminist. I don't even accept that I'm a feminist. I accept I'm an ordinary woman who is writing about what she knows. I try to project the image of women positively. I attempt to correct our men folks when they started writing, when they wrote little or less about women, when their female characters are prostitutes and ne'er do-wells. I started writing to tell them that this is not so. When I do write about women in Nigeria, in Africa, I try to paint a positive picture about women because there are many women who are very positive in their thinking, who are very, very independent, and very, very industrious.[6]

The major voice in African woman liberation movement is that of Buchi Emecheta who generalizes the eternal victimization of woman. She is the symbol of direct feminist protest. Greatly concerned about victimization and enslavement of traditional Igbo woman to the dictates of traditional Igbo culture, she raises her voice as a feminist. She vehemently protests against the deep-rooted notion that feminity and womanhood is sexuality and the ability to bear children and rearing them. Nnu Ego, Adah and Kehinde refuse to surrender to the Nigerian traditional mores. They are for the black woman empowerment. The feminism of Buchi Emecheta upheld the status of woman by contesting that woman is not merely an object meant for physical gratification and an industry for procreation.

Emecheta in her works is selective in choosing her personal experiences and general issues pertaining to African women to propound her "ism." She herself admits that for herself, she doesn't deal with great ideological issues. She writes about the little happenings of everyday life. Being a woman, and African born, she sees things through an African woman's eyes. She chronicles the little happenings in the lives of the African women she knows. She did not know that by doing so, she was going to be called a feminist. But if she is now a feminist then she is an African feminist with a small "f."

Flora Nwapa and Buchi Emecheta presented men in their writings in low profile, not of domineering nature. What is now needed of African writers, who write about contemporary woman, is a portrayal of promising woman that could become a model and to inspire Nigerian young women today. Though African woman mostly is a suffering woman, abused and discredited, she desires to marry a rich man who could provide her with all comforts in life.

The new African woman is visualized to be a professional woman, rational in her thinking, interested in her career and also conscious of her role as mother. For Nwapa motherhood is not only a phase in the life of woman to become complete woman but also a dimension of life even to disown fatherhood if necessary. And Emecheta gives much importance to motherhood, as woman becomes more inclined towards children especially sons. Nwapa and Emecheta show that professional women could not only make their career successful but also became good mothers.

Buchi Emecheta's novels have mirrored incidents in her own life. Her novel, *Second Class Citizen* speaks of her own experiences, her separation from her husband when he ventured to destroy the manuscript of her novel. But her children remained with her and her experiences in nurturing them formed the basis for the theme of her classic novel *The Joys of Motherhood.* In this novel, she emphasizes the importance of motherhood and children under her care. Nnu Ego's grandfather has no sons. Though his daughter, Ona is not traditionally married to Nwokocha Agbade, yet he prefers to send her to Agbade's house expecting that she would deliver a male child. But Ona dies after delivering Nnu Ego.

Nnu Ego becomes a fond mother of five sons but ultimately dies when her own educated sons abandon her. "She died quietly there by the roadside, with no child to hold her hand and no friend to talk to her. She had never really made many friends, so busy had she been building up her joys as mother."[7]

The intellectual, revolutionary and ideologue Ama Ata Aidoo aims at projecting a positive picture of womanhood. She is too bold to speak out openly the sensitivity of the social issues. Her feminism is an attempt to make women socially and politically conscious. She is not interested in focusing the traditional significance of her heroine as part of the mainstream of life. Nor does she allow her women protagonists become the victims of circumstances, as she hates the male dominance.

The women in the works of Ama Ata Aidoo are more radical compared to men and demonstrate solidarity with other women. The vengeful Esi and Sissie are such a pair. Ama Ata Aidoo in her theoretical essay "Unwelcome Pals and Decorative Slaves" has confessed that she is aware of the bitter criticism of her works that she has written like a man, outspoken, militant and vengeful.

Cyprian Ekwensi through his jaguar-like character Jagua in *Jagua Nana* launches an attack on the corrupt society. The reversal of the status of woman from secondary to primary is depicted vividly. Jagua stabilizes her position through prostitution, considering it to be similar to any other trade. Jagua considers prostitution as an authoritative independent trade a woman can run for herself. For her it signifies individuality, no mean business. And so she readily accepts money from Chief Ofubara rejecting even his marriage proposal.

> She felt rotten, loose and awful. She knew she could never really abandon her past life and settle down with someone like Chief Ofubara in village like Krinameh. But the money would come in useful. She reached out her hand and clasped the two bundles.[8]

There are different types of prostitution in vogue in African society encouraging poor women to become harlots, some to improve their economic status, as it is an instant-moneymaking enterprise and for the rich women to enrich themselves further through their contact and association with the affluent in the society. Mariama Ba is a crusader in her feministic approach, waging a battle against indignities inflicted upon women.

Chinua Achebe's women in his early works are plain, docile and indolent with no voice or involvement in serious activity. They are traditional and submit themselves to male supremacy. Even when the society is changing, they continue to be the same. Achebe has exposed the social immortality, sexual exploitation and ethnic bias in Nigeria. Female resistance shifts from trouble to a consensus, compromise and reconciliation. In *Things Fall Apart*, Ekwefi could not spell out her protest against the decision of the village elders, nor could she prevent Okonkwo from participating in the killing of Ikemefuana, a war hostage.

Nigerian authors like Chinua Achebe, Wole Soyinka and Cyprian Ekwensi portrayed women in the patriarchal society as having no individuality or freedom to enjoy power and lead their own life comfortably. But Flora Nwapa's women are progressive by their diligence, industry, ingenuity and resilience. They often wield power and protect themselves from humiliation and dehumanization unlike many of Buchi Emecheta and Mariama Ba's fictional heroines. Nwapa records traditional practices, which oppress women such as clitoridectomy, polygamy, wife inheritance and property disinheritance. She also challenges some of the fundamental assumptions concerning Igbo women's passively accepting retrogressive cultural norms.

Chidi Ikonne rightly remarks that "Nwapa's womenfolk are imbued with beliefs that mirror Ugwuta society. Her women passively accept the idea that 'woman' is basically inferior to man, a concept which underlies the folk attitude to and treatment of women."[9]

Wole Soyinka offers pigeonholed images of women, without significant feministic protest or voice raised against excesses of its male-dominated society. Except self-awareness, individual courage, integrity and moral austerity to a little extent, the women characters are not fully in the mould of feminism. Similarly, the other writers too hold different points of view while presenting the female characters.

It was believed in the traditional society that to beget a woman was to beget a man. Even an ugly girl does not become old at home. She shares the mysteries of life from beginning to end. Women were staunch supporters of husbands and active participants in religious activities. They used to share fortunes and misfortunes of man, family and society and carve a niche for themselves in the spiritual orientation. They were like the true fragrant flowers in the garden rendering life, pleasant and meaningful. They were the good omen for the family and the society. Women goddesses dominated the spiritual world of Africa more than the male gods. Women thus represent the more privileged class of society reflecting various aspects of the deities worshipped by the society.

Lake Goddess of Ugwuta oral traditions, 'Chi' personal spirit of Igbo society, Chielo, the priestess of the Oracle of Hills and the Caves, Mamiwata and Uhamiri of Nigerian society are the fount of feminity, courage, wealth, beauty, fertility and motherhood. They constitute the spiritual force and the people worship them for family welfare and prosperity. Some women are preachers, priestesses and also witch doctors believed to possess the mystical powers.

On the other hand, the treatment meted out to the widows and the widowers is alike. The period of mourning for a man after his death is at least three months during the period of which his widows in polygamous society must remain indoors. A widow neither bathes nor would plait her hair, nor change her clothes, which she had put on at the time of her husband's death. Similarly a widower will remain unwashed and unshaven during the period of mourning. Afterwards, the widow and widower are forced to put on their best clothes, sing, and dance and visit their friends, to thank them for condolences expressed on the death of their spouses.

Contrary to the status enjoyed by woman in the traditional Africa, the woman of modern Africa has to experience a lot of physical suffering as well as agony caused by ill-treatment and deprivation which lead to the emergence of feminism. In the beginning men and women shared the burden of their task in agriculture and trading. There was a common understanding between men and women to work together for betterment of family and society and to fight against corruption and other social evils. In doing so, men turned out to be organizers and working only for limited hours and thus overburdening women with the greater part of work initiated.

Some of the intellectual women felt insulted when they were considered inferior to men and demanded equality and parity. This led to the emergence of women liberation movement in the first decade of the twentieth century for uplift of women for equal rights, personal freedom, and economic independence and for parity and sexual emancipation. Men instead of giving better treatment to women turned more partial and prejudiced and started humiliating them by racism and sexism. The continuous conflicts on physical as well as emotional planes formed subjects of great concern for the writers within and outside the country. Such writers that would plead and advocate equal rights for women and parity with men are branded as 'feminist writers'.

The feminism in the West African novel is the call given by black women writers by addressing themselves to the grievances of black women in the contemporary African society. The justification of the influence of feminism lies in the emergence of a transformed society where the black woman has the least to grudge or grumble against her counterpart and her society. Though the desired effect could not be achieved immediately, the West African novel is sure to have paved the way for the transformation of agrarian society to exhibit equanimity, solidarity and woman fully co-operating with men and their society. The West African fiction shouldering a vital social responsibility has endeavoured to bring awareness among women for resurgence and renovation of society. Let us hope that the accomplishment of establishing an idealized society in conformity with the expectations of the African feminist writers does not remain a distant dream.

NOTES

1. Alice Walker, *In Search of Our Mother's Gardens* (London: The Women's Press, 1983).

2. Akpayom Imoh, "I Hate Being a Girl," *The Voice* (An Annual Magazine of the Press Club, Federal Government College), Ikot Ekpene, CRS, 1982-83 Session, Vol. II, p. 37.
3. Zaynab Alkali, "Feminist Propagandist," Interview with Quality Magazine Published on August 25, 1988.
4. Chinua Achebe, *Girls at War and Other Stories* (1972).
5. Umeh Marie, "The Poetics of Economic Independence for Female Empowerment: An Interview with Flora Nwapa (Special Issue on Flora Nwapa), Volume 26, *Research in African Literatures*, 6-1-1995.
6. Umeh Marie, 22 (8).
7. Buchi Emecheta, *The Joys of Motherhood*, (London: Heinemann, 1978), p. 224.
8. Cyprian Ekwensi, *Jagua Nana*, (London: Heinemann, 1951), p. 95.
9. Chidi Ikonne, "The Folk Roots of Flora Nwapa's Early Novels," *African Literature Today*, 18 (1992), pp. 96-104.

Select Bibliography

Primary Sources

Nwapa, Flora. *Efuru*, London: Heinemann, 1966.

_____. *Idu*, London: Heinemann, 1970.

_____. *One is Enough*, Enugu: Tana, 1981.

Emecheta, Buchi. *Destination Biafra*, London: Heinemann, 1982.

_____. *Second Class Citizen*, London: Fontana, 1977.

_____. *The Bride Price*, New York: George Braziller, 1976.

_____. *The Joys of Motherhood*, New York: George Braziller, 1979.

_____. *The Slave Girl*. New York: George Braziller, 1979.

Aidoo, Ama Ata. *Anowa*, London: Longman, 1970.

_____. *Changes: A Love Story*, London: Women's Press, 1991.

_____. *Our Sister Killjoy*, London: Longman, 1979.

_____. *The Dilemma of the Ghost*, London, Accra: Longman, 1965.

Secondary Sources

Achebe, Chinua. *A Man of the People*, New York: John Day, 1966.

_____. *Anthills of Savannah*, London: Heinemann, 1987.

_____. *Arrow of God*, New York: John Day, 1964.

_____. *No Longer at Ease*, London: Heinemann, 1963.

_____. *Things Fall Apart*, London: Heinemann, 1958.

Allan, Tuzyline. *Afterward. Changes: A Love Story*. New York: Feminist Press at CUNY, 1993.

Aluko, T.M. *One Man, One Wife*, London: Heinemann, 1967.

Amadi, Elachi. *The Concubine*, London: Heinemann, 1966.

Aidoo, Ama Ata. *Every Thing Counts*, No Sweetness Here, London: Longman, 1970.

_____. *Someone Talking to Someone*, Harare, Zimbabwe: College Press, 1985.

_____. "The African Woman Today." *Dissent* 39 (Summer 1992).

Andrade, Susan Zulema. *African Fictions and Feminisms: Making History and Remaking Traditions*. Diss. University of Michigan, 1993.

Asia, ed. Susheila Nasta. London: The Women's Press 1991, 3-23.

Awoonor, Kofi. *The Breast of the Earth*, New York: 1975.

Bakr, Abu Rashidah Ismaili (2001). West African Women in Exile: City, University and Dislocated Village. *Jenda: A Journal of Culture and African Women Studies*, 1, 1.

Ba, Mariama. *So Long a Letter*, Oxford: Heinemann, rpt. 1989.

_____. *Scarlet Song*, England: Longman, 1981.

Bamgbose, Ayo, Ayo Banjo and Andrew Thomas, ed. *New Englishes: A West African Perspective*. Trenton, NJ: Africa World P, 1997.

Barthelemy, Anthony. "Western Time, African Lives: Time in the Novels of Buchi Emecheta," *Callaloo*, 12.3 (1989), 559-74.

Bazin, Nancy Topping. *Feminist Perspectives in African Fiction*: Bessie Head and Buchi Emecheta. Black Scholar. 17.2 (1986): 34-40.

Beier, Ulli. *Introduction to African Literature*; an Anthology of Critical Writing from Black Orpheus. Evanston: Northwestern U P, 1967.

Berrian, Brenda F. "The Afro-American-West African Marriage Question: Its Literary and Historical contexts." *African Literature Today*, 1987.

_____. "African Women as Seen in the Works of Flora Nwapa and Ama Ata Aidoo." *College Language Association Journal*, 25.3 (1982).

_____. *Bibliography of African Women Writers and Journalists. Ancient Egypt-1984*. Washington D.C.: Three Continents, 1985.

Boehmer, Elleke Deirdre. *Mothers of Africa: Representations of Nations and Gender in Postcolonial African literature*. Diss. University of Oxford, 1990.

_____, "Stories of Women and Mothers: Gender and Nationalism in the Early Fiction of Flora Nwapa," *Motherlands: Black Women's Writing from Africa, the Caribbean and South*, ed. Susheila Nasta.

Boehmer, Elleke. "Of Goddesses and Stories: Gender and a New Politics in Achebe's *Anthills of the Savannah*." *Chinua Achebe: A Celebration*, ed. Kirstin Holst Peterson and Anna Rutherford. Oxford: Heinemann, 1990.

Booker, M. Keith. *The African Novel in English: An Introduction*. Portsmouth, NH: Heinemann, 1998.

Booth, James. *Sexual Politics in the Fiction of Ama Ata Aidoo*. Commonwealth Essays and Studies. 15.2 (1993): 80-96

Bose, Brinda. *Re-writing the Empire: Gender, Race and Silence in Colonial and Postcolonial Fiction*. Diss. Boston University, 1995.

Boserup, Ester, *Women's Role in Economic Development*. New York: Saint Martin's, 1970.

Brians, Paul. *Buchi Emecheta: The Joys of Motherhood.* Washington State University, 1996.

Brown, Lloyd Wellesley. *Women Writers in Black Africa.* West Port, CT: Greenwood Press, 1981.

Bruner, Charlotte H., ed. *The Heinemann Book of African Women's Writing*, Portsmouth, N H: Heinemann, 1993.

_____ and David Bruner, "Buchi Emecheta and Maryse Conde: Contemporary Writing from Africa and Caribbean," *World Literature Today*, 59 (1985) 9-13.

Bush, Barbara. *Slave Women in Caribbean Society*. Bloomington: Indiana University Press, 1990.

Chapman, Karen C. "Introduction to Ama Ata Aidoo's Dilemma of a Ghost." *Sturdy Black Bridges*, ed. Roseann P. Bell, Bettye J. Parker and Beverly Guy-Sheftall. Garden City, NY: Anchor Books, 1979.

Chetin, Sara. "Reading from a Distance: Ama Ata Aidoo's Our Sister Killjoy." *Black Women's Writing*, ed. Gina Wisker. New York: St. Martin's, 1993. 146-59.

Christian, Barbara. *Black Feminist Criticism.* New York, Penguin, 1986.

_____. "Alternate Visions of the Gendered Past: African Women Writers vs. Illich." *Feminist Issues*.3.1 (1983).

Cook, David. *African Literature: A Critical Review*, London: Longman, 1979.

Cox, Brian C., ed. *African Writers.* New York: Charles Scribner's, 1997.

D'Almeida, Irene Assiba, *Francophone Woman Writers: Destroying the Emptiness of Silence*. Gainesville: UP of Florida, 1994.

Dangarembga, Tsitsi. *Nervous Conditions*. Seattle: Seal Press, 1988.

Dathorne, O.R. *African Literature in the Twentieth Century*, London: Heinemann, 1975.

Davies, Carole Boyce. *Black Women, Writing and Identity: Migrations of the Subject*. New York: Routledge, 1994.

_____. "Introduction: Feminist Consciousness and African Literary Criticism," *Ngambika: Studies of Women in African Literature*, ed. Carole Boyce Davies and Anne Adams Graves. Trenton, NJ: Africa World Press, 1986. 1-23.

_____ and Elaine Savory Fido. *African Woman Writers: Toward a Literary History. A History of 20th Century African Literatures*, ed. Owomoyela Oakon. Lincoln and London: University of Nebraska Press, 1993.

Donatus, Nwaga, "The West Africa," *The Journal of CWL*, December 1967, No. 4.

Draper, James P., ed. *Black Literature Criticism: Excerpts from Criticism of the Most Significant Works of Black Authors over the Past 200 Years*. Detroit: Gale Research, 1992.

Ekwensi, Cyprian. *Jagua Nana*, London: Panther Books, 1961.

_____. *Jagua Nana*. London: Heinemann, 1975.

Elder, Arlene. "Ama Ata Aidoo and the Oral Tradition: A Paradox of Form and Substance." *African Literature Today*. 15 (1987): 109-18.

Emecheta Buchi, *Feminism with a Small f: Criticism and Ideology* ed. Kirstin Holst Peterson.

Emenyonu, Ernest. *The Rise of the Igbo Novel*, Ibadan: OUP, 1978.

_____. *The Journal of Commonwealth Literature*, Vol. XXI, No. 2, 1986.

Evans, Jennifer. "Women and Resistance in Ngugi's *Devil on the Cross*," *African Literature Today*. Trenton, New Jersey: African World Press, 1987.

Ezen, wa-Ọhaeto, "The Child Figures and Childhood Symbolism in Flora Nwapa's Children's Fiction" (Special Issue on Flora Nwapa) Vol. 26, *Research in African Literatures*, 6-1-1995, p. 68 (12).

Femi, Ojo-Ade, *Female Writers, Male Critics in Africa Literature Today*, London, Heinemann, 1983.

Figueroa, John J., ed. *An Anthology of African and Caribbean Writing in English*. London: Heinemann Educational Books in association with the Open University, 1982.

Fleming, Robert, ed. *After Hours: A Collection of Erotic Writing by Black Men*, New York: Penguin 2002.

Frank, Katherine. "Women without Men: The Feminist Novel in Africa." *African Literature Today*. 15 (1987).

Fredrickson, George, M. *Black Liberation: A Comparative History of Black Ideologies in the United States and South Africa*. New York: OUP. 1995,

Gardner, Susan, "The World of Flora Nwapa," *Women's Review of Books*, Volume XI, 3.1.1994, 9

Gikandi, Simon, ed. *Encyclopedia of African Literature*. London: Routledge, 2003.

Herdeck, Donald E. *African Authors; A Companion to Black African Writing*. Washington: Black Orpheus, 1973.

Heywood, Christopher. *Perspectives on African Literature*, London: Heinemann, 1979.

Human Rights Watch Report—June 2001: In the Shadow of Death: HIV/AIDS and Children's' Rights in Kenya.

Human Rights Watch Report on Women's Property Rights Violation in Kenya.

Human Rights Watch Report—Humanity Denied: Systematic Violation of Women's Rights in Afghanistan: October 2001.

Human Rights Watch Report;' New York, March 4, 2004.

Hunter, Jeffrey W. and Jerry Moore, ed. *Black Literature Criticism: Excerpts from Criticism of the Most Significant Works of Black Authors over the Past 200 Years: Supplement.* Detroit: Gale, 1999.

Hurston, Zora Neale. *Their Eyes Were Watching God.* New York: Harper and Roco, 1990.

Jahn, Janheinz. *Munto: African Culture and the Western World.* New York: Grove Weidenfeld, 1990.

_____. *A Bibliography of Neo-African Literature from Africa, America, and the Caribbean.* New York: F.A. Praeger, 1965.

_____, Ulla Schild and Almut Nordmann. *Who's Who in African Literature: Biographies, Works, Commentaries.* Tübingen: H. Erdmann, 1972.

_____ and Claus Peter Dressler. *Bibliography of Creative African Writing.* Nendeln, Liechtenstein: Kraus-Thomson, 1971.

James, Adeola. *In Their Own Voices: African Women Writers Talk.* Portsmouth, NH: Heinemann, 1990.

Jell-Bahlsen, Sabin. "Female Power: Water Priestesses of the Oru Igbo." *Sisterhood, Feminisms and Power*, ed. Obioma Nnaemeka, Lawrenceville, NJ: Africa World 1995.

Johnson, Rotimi. "Womanism and Feminism in African Letters," *The Literary Criterion*, 25.2 (1990).

Kanwar, Asha. "The Joys of Motherhood or the Sorrows of Otherhood." *Africa Quarterly*. 34.3 (1994): 54-63.

Katherine, Frank. "Women without Men: The Feminist Novel in Africa," *African Literature Today*, 15 (1987).

Katrak, Ketu H. "Womanhood/Motherhood: Variations on a Theme in Selected Novels of Buchi Emecheta," *The Journal of Commonwealth Literature*, 22.1 (1987): 159-70.

Article by Kidd, Devvy, an Advisory Board Member for the Wallace Institute, Founder and Director of Project on Winning Economic Reforms.

Keith, Booker. *The African Novel in English: An Introduction. Studies in African Literature*. New York: Heinemann, 1998.

Khayoom, S.A. *The Neo-Anthropological Novels of Chinua Achebe*. New Delhi: Prestige.

Killam, Douglas and Ruth Rowe, ed. *The Companion to African Literatures*. Bloomington: Indiana UP, 2000.

Klíma, Vladimír, Karel Frantisek Ruzicka and Petr Zima. *Black Africa: Literature and Language*. Dordrecht, Holland: D. Reidel, 1976.

Kulkarni, Harish. *Voices of Black Feminism: The Novels of Paule Marshall*. Aurangabad: Rajat, 1999.

Kwaku, Larbi Korang, "Ama Ata Aidoo's Voyage Out: Mapping the Coordinates of Modernity and African Selfhood in *Our Sister Killjoy*." (Unpublished essay, 1992).

Lang, D.M. and D.R. Dudley, ed. *The Penguin Companion to Classical, Oriental & African Literature*. New York: McGraw-Hill, 1971.

Lenta, Margaret. "The Need for Feminism: Black Township Writing," *Journal of Literary Studies*, 1988.

Lindfors, Bernth, ed. *Critical Perspectives on Nigerian Literatures*. Washington: Three Continents, 1976.

______ and Bala Kothandaraman. *South Asian Responses to Chinua Achebe*. New Delhi: Prestige.

_____ and Reinhard Sander, eds. *Twentieth-century Caribbean and Black African Writers. Third Series*. Detroit: Gale, 1996.

Mazrui, Ali A. "The Black Woman and the Problem of Gender: An African Perspective." *Research in African Literatures*. 24.1 (1993).

Mccaffrey, Kathleen. "Images of Women in West African Literature and Film: A Struggle against Dual Colonization," *International Journal of Women's Studies*, 1980.

Minh-ha, Trinh T. *Women, Native, Other Writing: Postcoloniality and Feminism*. Bloomington: Indiana OUP, 1980.

Mohanty, Chandra Talpade. "Under Western Eyes: Feiminist Scholarship and Colonial Discourses," *Boundary*, 2 .12 (1984), 333-40.

Mojola, Yemi, ed. "Flora Nwapa." *Perspectives on Nigerian Literature*: 1700 to the Present, Volume 2, p. 1.

Murray, Pauli, *The Liberation of Black Women: A Feminist Perspective*, ed. Jofreeman, California: Meyfield, 1975.

Nasta, Susheila, ed. *Motherlands: Black Women's Writing from Africa, the Caribbean, and South Asia*. New Brunswick, NJ: Rutgers UP, 1992.

Ngcobo, Lauretta. *The African Woman Writer, A Double Colonization: Colonial and Postcolonial Women's Writing*. Mundelstrup, Denmark: Dangaroo, 1986.

Njoku, Teresa U. "Womanism in Flora Nwapa's *One Is Enough* and *Women Are Different*." *Commonwealth Quarterly*, 14.39.

Nnaemeka, Obioma. "From Orality to Writing: African Women Writers and the (Re) Inscription of Womanhood." *Research in African Literatures*, 25 (Winter 1994), 137-57.

Nwankwo, Chimalum. "The Feminist Impulse and Social Realism in Ama Ata Aidoo's *No Sweetness Here* and *Our Sister Killjoy*." *Ngambika: Studies of Women in African Literature*, ed. Carole Boyce Davies and Anne Adams Graves. Trenton, NJ: Africa World Press, 1986. 151-59.

Ogunyemi, Chikwenye Okonjo. *Women and Nigerian Literature, Perspectives on Nigerian Literature*. Volume I. Lagos, Nigeria: Guardian Books, 1988.

_____. "Womanism: The Dynamics of the Contemporary Black Female Novel in English." *Signs: Journal of Women in Culture and Society*, 11.1 (1985): 63-80.

_____ and Marie Umeh, *Research in African Literatures*, Vol. 26, No. 2, Summer 1995. Special Issue: Flora Nwapa.

Ojo-Ade, Femi, "Women and the Nigerian Civil War: Buchi Emecheta and Flora Nwapa," (Journal Article) *Etudes, Germano-Africaines: Annual Review*, 6: 75.86, 1988. Waltham, M.A.

Oku, Julia Inyang Essien. "Courtesans and Earthmothers: A Feminist Reading of Cyprian Ekwensi's *Jagua Nana's Daughter* and Buchi Emecheta's *The Joys of Motherhood*." *Critical Theory and African Literature*, ed. Ernest N. Emenyonu, R. Vanamali, E. Oko, and A. Iloeje. Ibadan: Heinemann, 1987.

Osa, Osayimwense. "Buchi Emecheta's Feminism." *Literary Half-Yearly*. 31.1 (1990).

Owusu, Kofi. "Canons under Siege: Blackness, Femaleness, and Ama Ata Aidoo's *Our Sister Killjoy*," *Callaloo*. 13.2 (1990): 341-63.

Palmer, Eustace. *The Growth of the Novel*, London: Heinemann, 1979.

Perry, Alison. "Meeting Flora Nwapa," (Journal Article) *West Africa*, 3487: 1262, 1984 June 18, London, England.

Philips, Maggi, "Engaging Dreams: Alternative Perspectives on Flora Nwapa, Buchi Emecheta, Ama Ata Aidoo, Bessie Head and Tsits Dangarebga's Writing," *Research in African Literatures*, 25 (Winter 1994), 89-103.

Ponnumburisarvan, Charles. "Feminism and African Fiction: The Novels of Mariama Ba," *Modern Fiction Studies*, Vol. 34, No. 3, Autumn 1988.

Reddy, Indrasena. *The Novels of Achebe and Ngugi*. New Delhi: Prestige.

Research in African Literatures, Winter 1993, Vol. 24, No. 4.

Rosalyn Terborg-Penn, Sharan Healay, Andrea Rushing, *Women in Africa and the African Diaspora*, Washington: Howard University Press, 1987.

Roseae, A. *Mother is God: A Study in West African Literature*: London: Cambridge University Press, 1971.

Schipper, Mineke. "Emerging from the Shadows: Changing Patterns in Gender Matters," *Research in African Literatures*, 1996.

Smith, Bonnie G. "Changing Lives," *Women in European History since 1700* Lexington, M.A.D.C. Heath, 1989.

Soyinka, Wole. *The Interpreters*. London: Fontana, 1970.

Serafin, Steven R. *Modern Black Writers*, New York: The Continuous Publishing Co.

St. Peter, Christine. "Changing Worlds: The Nigerian Novels of Buchi Emecheta." *Atlantis*. 11 (Fall 1985):

Stratton, Florence. *Contemporary African literature and the Politics of Gender*. London: Routledge, 1994.

_____. "The Shallow Grave: Archetypes of Female Experience in African Fiction." *Research in African Literatures*, 1988.

Strategic Action Issue Area: African Women's Rights, ANC Historical Documents, Sep.1988.

Taiwo, Oladele. *Female Novelist of Modern Africa*: New York: St. Martin's Press, 1985.

Thiong'o, Ngugi wa. *Petals of Blood*, London: Heinemann, 1977.

_____. *Devil on the Cross*, London: Heinemann, 1982.

Umeh, Marie, "A Comparative Study of the Idea of Motherhood in Two Third World Novels," *CLA Journal*, 31.1 (1987) 343 Interview with Flora Nwapa.

_____. "The Poetics of Economic Independence for Female Empowerment." An Interview with Flora Nwapa. *Research in African Literatures*, 26 (2): 22-29, 1995, Summer.

Verba, Sharon. *Feminist and Womanist Criticism of African Literature: A Bibliography*. July 20, 1997.

Walsh, William. *Commonwealth Literature*. Oxford: OUP, 1973.

Wehrs, Donald R. *African Feminist Fiction and Indigenous Values*. Gainesville: U P of Florida, 2001.

Wilentz, Gay. Binding Cultures: *Black Women Writers in Africa and Diaspora*. Bloomington: Indiana University Press, 1992.

Wright, Edgar ed.: *The Critical Evaluation of African Literature*, London: Heinemann, 1973.

"From Orality to Writing; African Women Writers and the Reinscription of Womanhood," *Research in African Literatures*, Vol. 25, No. 4, Winter 1994.

"Mother Africa on a Pedestal: The Male Heritage in African Literature and Criticism," *African Literature Today*. 1987.

America's Working Women: A Documentary History 1600 to the Present. Rev. and updated ed.1995.

Imperial Leather; Race, Gender, Sexuality in the Colonial Context, N.Y.: Routledge, 1995.

Art, Dialogue and Outrage: Essays on Literature and Culture, Ibadan, Nigeria; New Horn Press, 1988.

Zell, Hans M., Carol Bundy, and Virginia Coulon, ed. *A New Reader's Guide to African Literature*. 2nd rev. ed. New York: Africana, 1983.

Interviews

Modebe, Sarah. "Remembering Tomorrow," A Conversation with Ama Ata Aidoo. *African Woman*. 5 (Autumn 1991): 31-33.

Maja-Pearce, Adewale. "We Were Feminists in Africa First." Interview. *Index on Censorship*. 19.9 (1990): 17-18.

McGregor, Maxine. *African Writers Talking*, ed. Dennis, Duerdon and Pieterne Cosmo, London, Heinemann, 1978-18.